Day by Day with God

September–December 2000

Day by Day with God

Bible Readings for Women

SEPTEMBER–DECEMBER 2000

Christina Press
Bible Reading Fellowship
Crowborough/Oxford

BRF, Peter's Way, Sandy Lane West, Oxford, OX4 5HG

First published in Great Britain 2000

ISBN 1 84101 130 4

Jacket design: JAC Design for Print, Crowborough

Trade representation in UK:
Lion Publishing plc, Peter's Way, Sandy Lane West,
Oxford OX4 5HG

Distributed in Australia by:
Willow Connection, PO Box 288, Brookvale, NSW 2100.
Tel: 02 9948 3957; Fax: 02 9948 8153;
E-mail: info@willowconnection.com.au

Distributed in New Zealand by:
Scripture Union Wholesale, PO Box 760, Wellington
Tel: 04 385 0421; Fax: 04 384 3990; E-mail: suwholesale@clear.net.nz

Distributed in South Africa by:
Struik Book Distributors, PO Box 193, Maitland 7405
Tel: 021 551 5900; Fax: 021 551 1124; E-mail: enquiries@struik.co.za

Acknowledgments

Scriptures quoted from the Good News Bible published by The Bible
Societies/HarperCollins Publishers Ltd, UK © American Bible Society
1966, 1971, 1976, 1992, used with permission.

The Living Bible copyright © 1971 by Tyndale House Publishers.

Scriptures from The New Revised Standard Version of the Bible,
Anglicized Edition, copyright © 1989, 1995 by the Division of
Christian Education of the National Council of the Churches of
Christ in the USA, used by permission. All rights reserved.

Scriptures from The Revised Standard Version of the Bible, copyright
© 1946, 1952, 1971 by the Division of Christian Education of the
National Council of the Churches of Christ in the USA, used by
permission. All rights reserved.

Scripture quotations taken from *The Holy Bible, New International
Version*, copyright © 1973, 1978, 1984 by International Bible Society.
Used by permission of Hodder & Stoughton Ltd. All rights reserved.
'NIV' is a registered trademark of International Bible Society. UK
trademark number 1448790.

Extracts from the Authorized Version of the Bible (The King James
Bible), the rights in which are vested in the Crown, are reproduced by
permission of the Crown's Patentee, Cambridge University Press.

The Message © 1993 by Eugene H. Peterson, NavPress, Colorado
Springs

Extract from 'Great is thy faithfulness' by William Runyan
(1870–1957)/Thomas O. Chisholm (1866–1960) copyright © 1951
Hope Publishing. Administered by CopyCare, P.O. Box 77, Hailsham
BN27 3EF, UK. Used by permission.

Printed in Great Britain
by Caledonian International Book Manufacturing Ltd, Glasgow

Contents

The Editor writes...

Today is one of those cold November days when I am glad I work at a desk in my own home and don't have to go out and face the chill north wind that is buffeting against my front door. In order to write this letter, I have been trying to think myself into September 2000, which is when you will be reading *Day by Day with God*. What will have happened in our world and in my life by then? Looking back a year can make us feel secure—it may have been a year full of happy times or a year of difficulties, but we are still here! We have survived and hopefully learned a little more about ourselves and about God's love for us.

Plans and hopes

But looking ahead? That is quite different! Mostly, life is so busy that we rush through each day trying to keep up with all the demands. A watch and a diary ensure we keep to schedule. We make plans and have hopes. We take it for granted that tomorrow will be there—but it may not be just as planned. Sandra Wheatley (Magazine section) has written honestly about how her future was completely shattered by the words of a hospital consultant. Life became, and still is, far from easy for her—and yet she is able to say that she has learned to be at peace and know that God is with her, keeping her safe and holding her close.

And that is how we all need to be able to view the future: that whatever lies ahead, God is with us—our strength, our comfort and our joy.

Living life to the full

This is one of the main aims of *Day by Day with God*—that what is written will help us to see how God is at work in his world and how we each have a part to play in his story. We are meant to live life to the full, whatever our circumstances, and for two weeks in November Dr Ann England guides our thoughts through what the Bible teaches us about wholeness. 'Learning to respond positively and creatively to life's experiences,' she writes, 'will help us grow into wholeness.'

Celia Bowring helps us to see what the Bible teaches about forgiveness, both to be able to accept forgiveness ourselves and to be able really to forgive those who have caused us pain in the past. This theme of forgiveness is picked up by Diana Archer in her note for 12 December, which tells us how Jesus challenges us to pray for our enemies. Through praying for those who have hurt us, we can be released from the anger and desire to hit back, and *really* forgive. Then, later in her notes, she quotes this verse from Jeremiah 29:11: '"For I know the plans I have for you," says the Lord, "plans to prosper you and not to harm you, plans to give you hope and a future."'

I have found this verse so helpful that I have written it on a card and pinned it on the wall to constantly reassure me when I wonder what lies ahead.

I trust that you, too, will find something in these pages, as you read them day by day, that will help you to live your life to the full, secure in the knowledge that God is the same yesterday, today and for ever.

Mary Reid

P.S. Thank you for the many letters that have arrived on my desk with words of encouragement, comments and ideas. Do keep writing: it helps me as I begin to plan the next year of notes for *Day by Day with God.*

Contributors

Beryl Adamsbaum is a language teacher living in France, just across the border from Geneva, Switzerland, where she and her husband have been engaged in Christian ministry for thirty years. She is involved in teaching, preaching and counselling. She is the editor of her church magazine and writes short devotional articles.

Diana Archer has three young children and a degree in religious studies, and has served in Japan as a missionary. She has worked in the publishing world as a freelance editor and writer. Her book *Who'd Plant a Church?* has been highly acclaimed.

Celia Bowring is the compiler of CARE's *Prayer Guide*, which highlights family and community issues and political and ethical concerns. Her recent book *The Special Years* is for parents of children under five. She works closely with her husband, Lyndon, in CARE, and is a contributor to several periodicals.

Ann England is a doctor who for some years worked as obstetrician and gynaecologist at Manorom, the Overseas Missionary Fellowship hospital in central Thailand. She was joint publisher of Christina Press with her husband Edward. She is a Trustee of Burrswood, a Christian centre for healing.

Rosemary Green has an international speaking ministry, sometimes alongside her husband Michael. Her highly praised book *God's Catalyst* distils her wisdom and experience gained through many years of prayer counselling. She is on the pastoral staff of Wycliffe Theological College in Oxford.

Margaret Killingray is a tutor at the London Institute for Contemporary Christianity. She has assisted Dr John Stott and others in running Christian Impact conferences here and overseas. Margaret and her husband, David, have three daughters and five grandchildren.

Christine Leonard lives in Surrey with her husband and two teenage children. She writes books for both adults and children; most tell the true stories of ordinary Christians who have done extraordinary things. She is the Vice President of the Association of Christian Writers.

Hilary McDowell is a deaconess in Belfast with a ministry of reconciliation and outreach through poetry, art, drama and music. Her book *Some Day I'm Going to Fly* has made her name known internationally. She has also written *On the Way to Bethlehem*, a book for Advent, and *Visit to a Second Favourite Planet*, both published by BRF.

Wendy Pritchard is the wife of John, Archdeacon of Canterbury. She is an enthusiastic part-time maths teacher, and mother of two daughters in their early twenties. Wendy has enjoyed each different phase of her life, from vicar's wife to mass caterer, and is interested in gardening, computing and solving life's problems.

Christina Rees was born in America and came to live in England twenty years ago when she met and married Chris Rees. She is a freelance writer and broadcaster, speaker, preacher and a member of the General Synod of the Church of England and the Archbishops' Council. She is also Chair of WATCH (Women and the Church), a national organization that provides a forum for promoting women in the Church.

Alie Stibbe has contributed to *Renewal* and other Christian publications. She lives at St Andrew's Vicarage, Chorleywood, where her husband Mark is the vicar. Previously they ministered in Sheffield. They have four children; the youngest is now at school.

Contributors are identified by their initials at the bottom of each page.

A Morning Prayer

Thank you, heavenly Father,
for this new day.
Be with me now
in all I do
and think
and say,
that it will be to your glory.

Amen

A sound from heaven

Suddenly a sound like the blowing of a violent wind came from heaven and filled the whole house where they were sitting... When they heard this sound, a crowd came together in bewilderment, because each one heard them speaking in his own language... 'We hear them declaring the wonders of God in our own tongues!'

Do you ever hear something which opens up a whole area and makes you think of things in a new way? A sermon on Acts 2 triggered that for me. Do read the whole chapter. As he discussed what sparks or prevents revival, the preacher said that sometimes God makes a sound from heaven and awaits our response. If it sounds like cynicism, apathy or grumbling, if we're too busy rushing around to listen to him, or deafened by the sounds of strife among ourselves, nothing much is going to happen.

Normally, God chooses to work with his people. In Acts they were 'together in one place', waiting for God, listening to him. Their response to the 'sound from heaven' was to 'declare the wonders of God'—and he in turn responded. I can picture him at a great 'mixing desk' in the sky, joyfully opening up the translation channels in a temporary reversal of Babel, ensuring that everyone in the mixed-race crowd understood the disciples' words in their own language. Three thousand people were added to the Church that day, and in a generation it had spread from Jerusalem to Rome.

The Bible has a good deal to say on God's voice and our response to it, about good sounds and bad sounds, about the kinds of sounds we make, the words that come out of our mouths, their tone as well as their content. We'll be looking at this together over the next few days.

God, I long to see you move in power; I long to see lives transformed. Help me to tune in to the sounds of heaven and to sing along in harmony so that your love songs are broadcast loud on earth.

CL

Hearing God-sounds

The heavens declare the glory of God; the skies proclaim the work of his hands. Day after day they pour forth speech; night after night they display knowledge. There is no speech or language where their voice is not heard. Their voice goes out into all the earth, their words to the ends of the world.

Very few are privileged to hear mighty rushing winds and see tongues of fire, so what are all these sounds from heaven? Well, for a start, wasn't the universe created through a sound, through God's voice, speaking? Doesn't its beauty and order and creativity and abundance still speak to us of his character, every day and in every language, if we will only listen?

Staying out in the country, I rose early and felt unusually close to God as I strolled through woods full of birdsong. 'God meant us to walk and talk with him in such space and quietness and beauty!' I enthused to a friend on my return. 'Yes, but you know I remember waking in the bleakness of a Communist capital, thinking, where is God in all this?' she replied. 'Then, looking down on the racket of a building site I saw some girders making the shape of a cross and I thought, he's here too! He's still speaking!'

There's a story about two men walking down a New York street. 'Listen to that grasshopper!' said one, a country farmer. 'You can't possibly hear a grasshopper among all this noise!' objected the other. In reply, the farmer took a dime from his pocket and let it fall to the ground. A dozen heads turned. 'You hear what your ears are tuned to!' the farmer said, as he pointed out a grasshopper on a fruit and veg stall.

Let's listen now to the sounds of heaven and respond, echoing the final words of Psalm 19: 'May the words of my mouth and the meditation of my heart be pleasing in your sight, O Lord, my Rock and my Redeemer.'

                                                                    CL

Ungodly sounds

With the tongue we praise our Lord and Father, and with it we curse men, who have been made in God's likeness.

Good sounds carry consequences, according to James' famous chapter on the tongue. 'Peacemakers who sow in peace raise a harvest of righteousness' but 'envy and selfish ambition leads to disorder and every evil practice.'

Trawling a Bible concordance for bad sounds—words like grumble, deceit, gossip, boasting—I found a wealth of references for all of them. 'Reckless words pierce like a sword, but the tongue of the wise brings healing'; 'A perverse man stirs up dissension, and a gossip separates close friends' (Proverbs 12:18; 16:28). I kept coming across stories too. Humanity's arrogant declaration of self-sufficiency spurred direct action from God at Babel; so did Israel's constant grumbling in the desert and their cynicism when the spies returned from Canaan; so did Ananias' and Sapphira's lie. If you look up some of these words you'll see that God is very concerned about the sounds we make, and often they change the way he acts, for good or for ill. Being holy, he simply can't accept the kind of behaviour that mixes evil with good, as today's passage highlights. 'Can both fresh water and salt water flow from the same spring?' James asks.

Of course God forgives us and Jesus' blood covers all our sins, but if we want to see him work with and through us we need to want just as passionately to be holy, as he is holy. If we really want to see his kingdom come and his will done on earth, let's clean up our act.

God, you are so practical. Help me to be conscious of the sounds I make today; to think, before I open my big mouth, would Jesus say those words, in that way? Help me to ask him what sounds I can make in order to create a little bit of his peace and harmony in my home, my office or in my children's school.

                                                                CL

Singers and gatekeepers

*And on that day they offered great sacrifices, rejoicing because
God had given them great joy. The women and children also
rejoiced. The sound of rejoicing in Jerusalem could be heard
far away... They performed the service of their God and the
service of purification, as did also the singers and gatekeepers.*

One Sunday, not long after I had heard the sermon about
responding to the sounds of heaven, a group of young people
came to lead the service in our church. Some sported dreadlocks
and all wore clothes more appropriate to New Age travellers
than to churchgoers in respectable Surrey. They played a song
whose words and tune we knew, but utterly changed the
rhythm—which many found an unnerving experience. As for
the instruments they played—we didn't even know their names.

It soon became clear, though, that they loved Jesus—and were
responding to his love by passing it on to others. Some worked in
a night shelter for homeless people; one lived with a group of
travellers. Far from deafening their neighbours with gospel blasts,
they were simply coming alongside, loving people, asking and
answering honest questions, taking their music and the presence
of Jesus to Glastonbury and other festivals, 'dancing' to a rhythm
which people could understand. They were singers, making 'the
rejoicing in Jerusalem... heard far away', and gatekeepers, welcoming people to God's kingdom, showing that words like 'high'
and 'love' don't have to be about drugs or frenzied sex, and that
only by losing do you find yourself.

This group challenged me because they were marching to a
different drumbeat, in response to the sound of God's voice. Like
the disciples in Acts 2, they communicated with those of different 'languages' and cultures, not only through their words, music
and actions, but through a total lifestyle.

*Is God asking you to 'sing his sounds' to members of a culture group
near you, whether on the golf course, at the single parent group, or the
local soup-run? What would it cost to change your rhythms of life?*
CL

Opposite sounds

A gentle answer turns away wrath, but a harsh word stirs up anger.

At the age of twenty-four, Philippa Stroud started reaching out to homeless people in Bedford. Others from her church joined her, mainly young women at first. Inexperienced and working with men who were in and out of jail or mental hospital, or high on drink and drugs, they encountered violence daily at that time. I asked how none of them had received serious injuries. 'We prayed... and we found that the Bible is right when it says that a gentle answer stops anger in its tracks,' they replied.

A girl from my own church moved to a run-down inner-city estate, as part of a church-plant. Their strategy was to 'live in the opposite spirit'—to make new sounds which were changing the prevailing tune. So if they found lonely isolation, they would make the sounds of community—they would invite people round and give local children opportunities to play safely. If they heard the sounds of boredom they would introduce purpose, motivating people to improve their own environment, perhaps. If they heard arguments they would actively involve themselves, listening and becoming peacemakers. When they heard despair they came alongside individuals, bringing hope. They would regularly praise and worship God in the midst of the estate because they believed that sounds can transform a whole atmosphere. Psalm 89:15 (NRSV) says, 'Happy are the people who know the festal shout.' Isaiah 40:9 (NIV) says, 'Lift up your voice with a shout, lift it up, do not be afraid; say to the towns of Judah, "Here is your God!"'

Whether you live in the inner city or amid the materialism and apparent self-sufficiency of the suburbs, ask God to show you how to make his sounds, rather than the prevailing ones. In the words of Francis of Assisi: 'Where there is hatred, let me sow love; where there is injury, pardon; where there is doubt, faith; where there is despair, hope; where there is darkness, light; where there is despair, joy.'

CL

Love-sounds

If I speak in the tongues of men and of angels, but have not love, I am only a resounding gong or a clanging cymbal.

A violinist playing the right notes with the wrong tone or expression can make music feel and sound horrible. We can't cheat either. God knows when we're motivated by something other than his love and his Spirit. Even if we say and do the 'right things' his response from heaven won't be favourable.

God said to his prophet Ezekiel (33:31–32), 'My people come to you, as they usually do, and sit before you to listen to your words, but they do not put them into practice. With their mouths they express devotion, but their hearts are greedy for unjust gain. Indeed, to them you are nothing more than one who sings love songs with a beautiful voice and plays an instrument well, for they hear your words but do not put them into practice.' What sadness—God's sadness empathizing with his servant's sadness! Yet how often do we judge church services by whether we've been pleased or entertained? How often do we merely give assent or take comfort from the Bible instead of building our lives on its fundamentals—loving God and our neighbours?

As I was racing to finish writing this, at the end of a busy and emotionally draining day, an old lady phoned. Would I take her to an important church meeting that evening? With bad grace I agreed. It would mean leaving early. Normally my husband would drive, but he was visiting his mother in hospital. Bother, why couldn't someone else take her? I turned back to these notes. Oh dear! There are times when I'd rather not hear God's voice reminding me how often, when it's inconvenient or I'm upset or lacking in energy, I make excuses not to love people. Did five extra minutes, a smile and a listening ear really cost so very much?

Sorry… again! Help me be a sweet sound in your (and other people's) ears!

CL

'Let me hear your voice'

The trumpeters and singers joined in unison, as with one voice, to give praise and thanks to the Lord. Accompanied by trumpets, cymbals and other instruments, they raised their voices in praise to the Lord and sang: 'He is good; his love endures for ever.'

'I'm surprised you play the trumpet,' said an old friend to my husband, who'd recently dusted off his old school instrument and joined the church worship band. 'It's an extrovert's instrument, yet you've always served quietly, in the background.' 'Maybe, but there's nothing like it, playing with a group of worshipping people and letting rip!' I heard John reply.

Song of Songs 2:14 says, 'My dove in the clefts of the rock, in the hiding-places on the mountainside, show me your face, let me hear your voice; for your voice is sweet, and your face is lovely.' Any lover does long to hear his beloved's voice. As for God's own voice, Job 37:4 says, 'When his voice resounds, he holds nothing back.' Do we hold back in worship, hiding behind inhibitions or tradition, or can we find a way, a time, a place when we can 'let rip' with our praise to God? When we do, alone, or more especially with a group who are all 'lost in wonder, love and praise', doesn't something happen to us?

As Israel worshipped at the dedication of the new temple, something quite amazing happened. It 'was filled with a cloud, and the priests could not perform their service because of the cloud, for the glory of the Lord filled the temple of God.' When the sounds of earth join in concert with the sounds of heaven, who knows what may result?

Show me how to worship you with all my heart and mind and soul and strength, with every part of me, not holding anything back! As I find my own ways to do that, help me to join with others in such unison that our 'sound' will not only please heaven but affect this earth.

CL

Responding to God's voice

The sheep listen to his voice. He calls his own sheep by name and leads them out. When he has brought out all his own, he goes on ahead of them, and his sheep follow him because they know his voice.

God's voice, Revelation tells us, is like the thunder of many waters. What majesty and authority! Yet I'm really pleased that it's sheep who follow him. Such vulnerable creatures wouldn't run after a frightening person. Barking dogs might drive them, but they would only *follow* someone who led them to green pastures.

Just in case our arrogance assumes that our little flock alone truly hears his voice, he says, 'I have other sheep that are not of this sheep pen. I must bring them also. They too will listen to my voice, and there shall be one flock and one shepherd.' Sounds of unity among Christians will attract his blessing.

So, we're his sheep. Do we hear his voice? It's easy to think we don't because it has never thundered at us like many waters. Panic sets in. We can't be his sheep then! But, 'Whether you turn to the right or to the left, your ears will hear a voice behind you, saying, "This is the way; walk in it," ' Isaiah 30:21 tells us. Often we take for granted the fact that he is guiding us, quietly, gently. Only when we look back can we see the pattern of it. I wish he'd use—if not sky writing—fax or e-mail, but the fault is in my receiving rather than in his transmission. I take for granted those times he whispers to my conscience, helping me walk in his ways, because it all seems very nebulous. I have a feeling, though, that the more we obey, the more he will speak to us until, like Isaiah (6:8), we shall hear the voice of the Lord saying, 'Whom shall I send? And who will go for us?'

And I said, 'Here am I. Send me!'

CL

The gentle whisper

After the earthquake came a fire, but the Lord was not in the fire. And after the fire came a gentle whisper.

Elijah was good at hearing gentle whispers. He even heard rain that wasn't there, that hadn't been there during three years of drought. He heard it coming before (seven times before) his servant could see 'a cloud as small as a man's hand rising from the sea'. And sure enough, the drought broke, setting God's seal on the great miracle in which fire had consumed the water-soaked sacrifices along with all the wicked prophets of Baal. But then Elijah was a prophet, a proper prophet, so obviously it was easy for him.

But then the great prophet and national hero experienced burn-out. After all his triumphs he collapsed in a little heap, feeling sorry for himself. Dramatic earthquake and wind revived him, then a still small voice spoke to him. But so gentle a God gave no light commission. 'Go back the way you came, and go to the Desert of Damascus. When you get there, anoint Hazael king over Aram. Also, anoint Jehu son of Nimshi king over Israel, and anoint Elisha son of Shaphat from Abel Meholah to succeed you as prophet.' What was it in that still small voice, that presence, which revived a worn-out, frightened, lonely man and equipped him to carry out those epoch-making instructions?

When I catch a few notes of the sounds of heaven and try to respond, Lord, I often feel overwhelmed, as though I've found myself in the midst of some great orchestra clutching only a mistuned triangle and no sheet music! Help me to listen for the whisper of your still small voice which encourages me—gives me courage. Help me to straighten out my triangle and to hold it away from my own body, so that it rings out and rings true when my cues come, as they will—for you, the maker of the universe, live with and may choose to sing through me!

CL

Elijah confronts a king

Now Elijah… said to Ahab, 'As the Lord, the God of Israel, lives, whom I serve, there will be neither dew nor rain in the next few years except at my word.' Then the word of the Lord came to Elijah: 'Leave here, turn eastward and hide.'

The first book of Kings begins with the death of King David. It chronicles the kings from Solomon, David's son, through the division of the kingdom into two parts—northern Israel with its own kings and southern Judah with its capital, Jerusalem and another line of kings. It is not encouraging reading. These kings had the God-given task of leading the people of Israel in true worship and godly obedience. Most of them failed, turning to other gods, even serving one by sacrificing children to fire. Over and over again the words ring out as kings die—'He did evil in the eyes of the Lord.'

It is hard to challenge evil, especially when it is dangerous to do so. Elijah knew that challenging King Ahab, one of the worst of all the kings, could mean death. With his wife Jezebel, Ahab had gone further than any other king in turning to the god Baal. The Bible records God's fatherly patience with his disobedient people. He sends prophets to warn them of impending disaster. He sends enemy armies, drought and famine to shake them into repentance. Elijah's story begins with him telling Ahab that God's power is greater than any other god's, that a terrible drought has begun, and then he disappears hurriedly into the desert.

We see many examples in the news of men and women who feel called to challenge dictators, unjust systems and corrupt police. Britain is host to many who have fled to safety. But there are smaller challenges to face—unjust employers, bullying school fellows, prejudices of all kinds, gossip and rumour. Could we take our courage in both hands and stand up to someone? Like Elijah, we may one day know that God is calling us to do so.

MK

Elijah is encouraged

Elijah picked up the child and carried him down from the room into the house. He gave him to his mother and said, 'Look, your son is alive!' Then the woman said to Elijah, 'Now I know that you are a man of God and that the word of the Lord from your mouth is truth.'

Slowly over several years the Lord prepared Elijah, and the people of Israel under Ahab, for a massive confrontation, which we will read about tomorrow.

Elijah ran away from Ahab to camp in the open by a desert stream. There God cared for him, ravens bringing food, the brook providing water. But the drought continued and the brook dried up, and Elijah moved on into a country beyond Ahab's rule. There he met a widow, whose heart had been prepared by the Lord to welcome and care for Elijah, and who trusted God enough to feed him with her last little store of food although it brought death by starvation closer for her and her son (17:12). Twice God gave miracles that snatched life from death. He provided food for them during the famine (17:16), and when the widow's son fell ill and seemed to be dead, Elijah's anguished prayer brought him back to life (17:19–21).

The widow listened to Elijah and accepted his word from God. Her faith and the miracles encouraged Elijah. Now he was ready to return to hostility and danger, his faith in God's power renewed.

We need encouragers—friends who will take us in, feed us, pray with us and remind us of the love and power of our God. Some of us are very tempted to battle alone, even refusing help and love when it is offered. Perhaps the Lord is waiting to build you up in your faith and encourage you through the ministry of someone offering you a meal, a lift or a weekend away. Accept—and expect just a little miracle!

MK

Elijah faces the prophets of Baal

Elijah went before the people and said, 'How long will you waver between two opinions? If the Lord is God, follow him; but if Baal is God, follow him.' But the people said nothing.

On his return, Elijah discovers that the queen has killed many of the Lord's prophets. He challenges the servants of Baal to a contest. On Mount Carmel before all the people, Elijah brings wood and two bulls. Ahab assembles over four hundred prophets of Baal, who set up an altar with the wood and the meat of one bull.

'Call on the name of your god,' Elijah tells them, 'and I will call on the name of the Lord. The god who answers by fire—he is God' (18:24). All day Baal's prophets shout and dance round the altar; in a frenzy of frantic pleading, they cut and slash themselves. 'But there was no response, no one answered, no one paid attention' (18:29).

As the evening shadows lengthen, Elijah, on his own, prepares another altar, this time to the Lord, and puts on the wood and the meat. He increases the drama by soaking it all in water. Then he steps forward and simply prays—no ecstatic dancing, no frenzy—for God to send down fire 'so these people will know that you, O Lord, are God'. The fire comes, burning up the sacrifice, the wood, as well as the stones of the altar.

At the total victory of God, the people fall to the ground and cry, 'The Lord, he is God.' Elijah has defeated the servants of evil gods, and confounded the king in his idolatry. At last their eyes have seen the truth. However, reading on, we find that Ahab and Jezebel still bitterly oppose the Lord, and the people are soon wavering again.

Lord, help me to live by faith, not by sight. I long to experience your presence and power so that all doubt is removed. But I want to learn how to trust you through times of drought, when I cannot see.

MK

Elijah despairs

Elijah was afraid and ran for his life. 'I have had enough, Lord,' he said. 'Take my life.'

Elijah had been on the top of the mountain, his arms flung wide to the heavens in prayer, the people kneeling before him acknowledging God. But the unrepentant and angry queen still wants him dead.

We can be caught out by success and the high moments of life, expecting them to last and being devastated when they don't. On his own, in suicidal despair, Elijah sinks to his knees in the desert and falls asleep with a desperate prayer on his lips. It is worth reading verses 3–9 several times. Christians sometimes feel guilty when they experience suicidal depression. Yet some of us will. In this passage we can see the Lord accepting this weakness and caring for Elijah in gentle and practical ways. He doesn't tell him what to do—that comes later. He simply feeds him and lets him sleep. Then Elijah carries on with his wild flight. The Lord doesn't start telling him to go back until later in the chapter! He travels, strengthened mainly by food and sleep, brought not so much by prayer, nor directly by the Lord, nor by miracles, but by quiet, undemonstrative angels.

I can still remember dealing with a small child who was crying beyond all comfort. I sat beside her while she screamed and kicked, then I wiped her nose and eyes, gave her a drink, and eventually sorted out the problem. She had totally misunderstood something I had said to her. In tomorrow's reading the Lord begins to sort out Elijah's misunderstandings, but first he holds him, feeds him and is simply there.

Praise be to the God and Father of our Lord Jesus Christ, the Father of compassion and the God of all comfort, who comforts us in all our troubles, so that we can comfort those in any trouble with the comfort we ourselves have received from God (2 Corinthians 1:3–4).

MK

Elijah is told to go back

And the word of the Lord came to him: 'What are you doing here, Elijah?' … The Lord said to him, 'Go back the way you came.'

He had arrived at Mount Horeb far to the south, but Horeb is Sinai, the mountain where Moses received the Ten Commandments and God laid down the covenant terms of his relationship with the people of Israel. Now the Lord asks him what he is doing there, and Elijah cries out in despair that the covenant has been rejected, all the prophets of the Lord are dead, and he is the only one left. He only remembers the defeats; the triumph is forgotten.

The Lord now begins the process of 're-educating' Elijah. First he shows him that he is there with him, not in the 'earthquake, wind and fire', but in 'the sound of silence'. He is not just in the dramatic miracles. Then God asks him again what he is doing there. Like a sullen child, Elijah repeats his tale of woe. This time the Lord puts the record straight; telling him that there are seven thousand others who still serve the Lord in Israel, sending him to recruit two kings and a prophet who will carry on the task of defeating the servants of Baal. Elijah's role in the battle is now to hand on the fight to others. There are familiar echoes in the way that Elijah complained that he was the only prophet left, and then is rather reluctant to hand over to successors!

'Go back the way you came.' This journey was not necessary; it was not part of God's plan for Elijah. But the Lord did not abandon his servant, even using Elijah's rash and hasty escape to build a deeper relationship with him.

Christian leaders sometimes are tempted to think that only they can run things, and that everything will fall apart if they are not there. Pray for those you know who complain of overwork, but don't want to let go.

MK

Elijah confronts Ahab again

Ahab said to Elijah, 'So you have found me, my enemy!' 'I have found you,' he answered, 'because you have sold yourself to do evil in the eyes of the Lord. I am going to bring disaster on you.'

It is well worth reading this dramatic and appalling chapter. Ahab, the king, lies on his bed, sullen and angry and refusing to eat, because a man called Naboth won't sell him his vineyard. Jezebel, despising her weak and childish husband, tells him simply to take the vineyard. The Lord sends Elijah to confront Ahab.

Here we see a graphic illustration of God's commandments ignored and broken. Ahab begins by coveting the vineyard (commandment number 10); Jezebel's plot involves false testimony (number 9), misusing the Lord's name (number 3), murder (number 6) and theft (number 8). Moreover she misuses the king's power and authority to make others carry out the plot to murder Naboth.

Elijah's challenge and prophecy of disaster and violent death for both Ahab and Jezebel is so powerful that Ahab is humbled. His repentance delays until after his death the consequences of such evil.

Ahab was responsible for others; he was a leader who was expected to set a good example; he knew the right way to live and to lead, but he went the wrong way. He allowed himself to be led into very dark paths by his powerful and wicked wife. Jesus said, 'Things that cause people to sin are bound to come, but woe to that person through whom they come. It would be better for him to be thrown into the sea with a millstone tied round his neck than for him to cause one of these little ones to sin' (Luke 17:2).

Lord, help me never to cause someone else to stumble and sin, especially those who are younger or weaker than I am, or who look to me for guidance.

                                                                                    MK

Elijah appears with Jesus

[Jesus'] face shone like the sun, and his clothes became as white as the light. Just then there appeared before them Moses and Elijah, talking with Jesus.

The last prophet of the Old Testament, Malachi, had promised that Elijah would be sent by God one day to warn people of the coming kingdom of God. The followers of Jesus and of John the Baptist remembered Malachi's promise and wondered whether either of them was Elijah come back. There are many other references to Elijah in the New Testament. The angel who told John the Baptist's father that he would have a special son said that John would go on before the Lord in the spirit and power of Elijah, to make ready a people prepared for the Lord.

Elijah was a powerful prophet whose story reminds us that in our world today Christians face wicked and destructive leaders, just as he did. We need to remember to pray for those who have to stand up and challenge evil.

Elijah stood on the mountain top and knew the Lord's power, and then dropped right down on his knees in the desert, in deep depression. His story reminds us that our Lord knows what it feels like to be human, to be lonely, abandoned and to suffer, and because of that he knows how to comfort us.

Elijah appears with Moses the law-giver, as Jesus is transfigured, shining like the sun. Moses and Elijah were men, humans like us who need a redeemer, the eternal Son of God. This meeting on the mountain showed the disciples that Jesus was greater than all the heroes of Jewish history. It also tells us that, like them, we will be with him after death, fully ourselves.

Lord, help me to fight your battles, knowing that you are by my side, just as Elijah did. Help me to recognize evil and to know when you call me to stand up against it.

MK

Putting God first

Hezekiah trusted in the Lord, the God of Israel. There was no one like him among all the kings of Judah, either before him or after him. He held fast to the Lord and did not cease to follow him; he kept the commands the Lord had given Moses.

Hezekiah was king of the southern kingdom of Judah, a hundred years after Elijah. The four books of Kings and Chronicles tell the stories of the kings and the people, some choosing to ignore God, his love and his laws, and some choosing to worship and obey him. Hezekiah was one who chose to obey. Because he was a king, the leader of his nation, he wanted to encourage the people to follow him in obedience and worship. We may not be able to identify fully with a king of ancient Israel, but there are lessons we can learn from Hezekiah and his difficult discipleship in harsh times. His story is told in 2 Kings 18—20, 2 Chronicles 29—32 and Isaiah 36—39.

Shortly after he became king of the southern kingdom, the northern part, Israel, was conquered and many of the people taken into exile in Assyria. He was king of just the small area around Jerusalem, called Judah. Would they be next?

Hezekiah began his reign by restoring the true worship of God, getting rid of the altars to other gods. Even the bronze snake that Moses had made at God's command to save the people from a plague of poisonous snakes (Numbers 21:8), that Jesus used to illustrate his own death (John 3:14)—even such a 'holy' object as that, Hezekiah destroyed. He did it because they were worshipping the snake rather than God himself.

'Seek first God's kingdom and his righteousness' (Matthew 6:33). Everything else falls into place after that. Hezekiah did that and God honoured his faithfulness by helping him defeat his enemies and protect his land (2 Kings 18:1, 8).

What is most important in our lives? Do we seek him first? Are there ever 'good' things that come between us and our worship of the Lord? We need to ask these questions honestly.

MK

Making mistakes

This is what the great king, the king of Assyria, says: On what are you basing this confidence of yours? You say you have strategy and military strength—but you speak only empty words.

Chapter 18, verses 19–25, gives us the ultimatum that the king of Assyria's commander shouts at Hezekiah's officers so that all Jerusalem can hear. Seven years after the Northern Kingdom had been conquered, Assyria comes back to attack Hezekiah. Hezekiah tries to bribe the Assyrian king to go away, giving him gold and silver, some from the temple he had only recently repaired (18:16). When the Assyrians simply take the bribe and continue the attack, Hezekiah has to face his humiliation and admit his mistake. Decisions in life can sometimes be very difficult. Should Hezekiah have given the gold and silver to King Sennacherib? He was doing all he could to protect the land and the people. In 2 Chronicles 32:2–6 we read of the practical and military preparations he made. Mistakes are not always sin; they are the outcome of our limited understanding of circumstances and people. We are sometimes too quick to blame each other, and our leaders, for mistakes that are simply part of being human.

In the end it made no difference. He had to trust God to save them. Dealing with mistakes with honesty, putting them right, and admitting we were wrong are some of the hardest things we have to do, but they can be the beginning of a wonderful new relationship with the Lord, and with others. Reassuring someone, perhaps a close relative, that we understand and could just as easily have made the same mistake ourselves, can also be liberating.

'[Hezekiah] did what was right in the eyes of the Lord, just as his father David had done' (18:3). Of course, that doesn't mean he never did wrong, any more than David, but he knew what was right, and like David he found full forgiveness when he repented and turned to the Lord. Christian disciples are not the good, but the forgiven, and obey God out of love and gratitude.

MK

Praying in faith

Now, O Lord our God, deliver us from [Sennacherib's] hand, so that all kingdoms on earth may know that you alone, O Lord, are God.

'On what are you basing this confidence of yours?' the king of Assyria asks. 'Will your God rescue you when he did not rescue Israel? Surrender to me and you will not suffer.' As he reads the letter from Sennacherib, all Hezekiah can do is pray. He goes in repentant anguish to the temple, and sends his officials to Isaiah, the prophet, for a word from the Lord. Hezekiah knows that a miraculous rescue will demonstrate God's power, answering the Assyrian taunts that the Lord is powerless. Isaiah tells him not to be afraid because the Lord will deal with Sennacherib of Assyria.

How do we pray when crises overwhelm us? When we are powerless to avoid defeat? When we are terrified of tomorrow? We have to face the possibility that even with perfect trust in God, and a strong faith that he will work his purposes out, it does not necessarily mean that we will be rescued and that nothing terrible will happen to us. We know that it can and sometimes does happen.

In the book of Daniel three servants of God, Shadrach, Meshach and Abednego, are faced with a horrific death by fire. They too are taunted with the powerlessness of their God. They reply, 'If we are thrown in the fire, the God we serve is able to save us, but even if he does not, we want you to know that we still trust in him alone.' Now Hezekiah prays not knowing how it will work out, but in the end the Lord sent a plague and the Assyrians went home.

If we believe deep down that our lives and our times are in the Lord's hands, and that he is in control, then sometimes we will rejoice as we see him at work, but sometimes there will be hard things that we cannot understand. Pray for those you know who find life tough and difficult to understand.

MK

Starting again

Tell Hezekiah, the leader of my people, 'This is what the Lord, the God of your father David, says: I have heard your prayer and seen your tears; I will heal you.'

Poor Hezekiah had a boil and it was killing him. Isaiah told him to sort out his affairs and put everything in order for the next king. But the Lord responded to his tearful prayers and Isaiah came back with an ointment made of mashed-up figs—and a new message from the Lord. He had a second chance!

Someone I met recently, a happily married woman with two children, told me how she had lost her left leg. She had had a very aggressive cancer in her twenties and was given six months to live and told that the treatment would quite likely mean she would never have children. She faced death, and then was given back life and family. Not many of us have such a dramatic new start as she had, but her joy in living was an infectious and heart-lifting special gift to all she met.

Hezekiah was desperate to live, to finish the task of bringing the people back on the right paths. Through Isaiah God gave him a fresh start. The Lord promises him fifteen more years in a city protected from its enemies by the Lord's hand.

Many people long for a fresh start. Every new year is seen as a chance to start again, but it's a dream that soon fades. Being a Christian is about fresh starts, the one wonderful fresh start when we accept the forgiveness we are offered through the cross of Jesus. Then every day we can start again—of course, we have to live with our mistakes, even some painful ones, but each fresh day is a new day with the Lord, working for his kingdom, as Hezekiah did.

Did you start again this morning?

MK

Rejoicing and celebrating

The whole assembly then agreed to celebrate the festival seven more days; so for another seven days they celebrated joyfully.

Hezekiah's reign is recorded in 2 Chronicles, where the emphasis is on his reform and rebuilding of the temple and its regular pattern of worship. Long neglected by previous kings, Hezekiah decides to hold the feast of the Passover in Jerusalem. The Passover celebrated God's rescue of the people of Israel from slavery in Egypt long years before. Hezekiah invites not only the people of his own kingdom, but also the remnants of the northern Israelites, now under the rule of Assyria. He invites them to come as a way of saying sorry to God, a way of reconsecrating themselves to his service. Perhaps this turning back in repentance might lead to the restoration of the kingdom and the return of the exiles (30:9)? Some who came were willing but did not fully understand what it was all about. They had not prepared themselves properly, but Hezekiah prayed for them, asking the Lord to accept their praise, even though they were only just beginning to seek him.

This was a great party: there was singing and music, praise and prayer, feasting and fellowship. When it was due to end, they all agreed to carry on for another week. There had been nothing like it since the days of David.

When we remember the Lord's death in bread and wine at communion, we are following Jesus' instructions at the last supper when he turned the Passover into a new thanksgiving. Are Christians able, or even willing, to let their thanks and joy at being rescued spill over into quality time together, not just a couple of hours in church, but time to enjoy each others' company, eating and drinking together, mixing the age groups, crossing all the other barriers that divide us? And can we include the seekers, the questioners, the damaged who long to join in but don't fully understand what it is all about?

MK

Being sure of heaven

For the grave cannot praise you, death cannot sing your praise,
those who go down to the pit cannot hope for your faithfulness.
The living, the living—they praise you, as I am doing today.

I don't want to die. I certainly don't fancy the process, but I actually don't want to leave this world. I enjoy it most of the time and I want to see what happens. It is hard to imagine a world going on in the same old way without me here.

Hezekiah certainly did not want to die, and when he was given a new chunk of living he wrote down his thoughts in this poem of thanks and Isaiah passed it on to us.

The greatest difference between Hezekiah and me (and there are quite a few!) is that I am living after the resurrection of Jesus. I know that Jesus came back after death, that his friends recognized him. He cooked breakfast and ate with them. He told the thief who was executed with him that they would meet in paradise. I know that after death I will be in heaven. I can't imagine what that will be like, but there are enough hints for me to know that every experience of joy and beauty I have ever known will be multiplied a hundredfold.

Hezekiah was not at all certain about life after death. He believed that there was a place where the spirits of the dead went, but was not sure what kind of place it was. He wasn't even sure that God would be there to be praised as he could be by the living. He did not have our certainty.

Hezekiah began his poem with the words, 'In the prime of my life must I go through the gates of death and be robbed of the rest of my years?' Jesus died at thirty-three, having done all that he came to do. We know that our deaths do not rob us of lost years, but are the beginning of true fulfilment.

Are you sure of heaven? Read one of the accounts of the resurrection and let that give you assurance.

MK

Knowing God is in charge

Comfort, comfort my people, says your God. Speak tenderly to Jerusalem, and proclaim to her that her hard service has been completed, that her sin has been paid for.

Isaiah's account of Hezekiah's reign ends with a visit from some envoys from Babylon. Hezekiah gladly meets them and shows them all his royal treasures. But the Babylonians will be the next great power, taking over from Assyria. Isaiah warns him that it will be a Babylonian army that conquers Judah and brings total destruction to the kingdom.

Hezekiah's son, Manasseh, came to the throne at the age of twelve and reigned a long time. He turned away from God and 'shed so much innocent blood that he filled Jerusalem from end to end' (2 Kings 21:16). He made it even more certain that the prophesied doom and destruction would fall on Jerusalem, which happened in about 587BC. All the good that Hezekiah and Elijah had done did not last. Those who lived through it all must have despaired.

But Isaiah brings the promise of comfort, of an end to suffering and judgment. Some of the younger exiles lived to see the beginning of the return to the land of Israel, and later the temple was rebuilt. They saw Isaiah's words starting to come true. But Isaiah also spoke about a voice in the desert preparing the way for the Lord (40:3). These verses were remembered with joy when John the Baptist came to prepare the way for Jesus.

Many of the promises in the Bible come true in stages, partly at the time they were spoken, partly in the future, and completely when the Lord comes again and all promises are fulfilled in Jesus the triumphant king. Hezekiah sought to worship and obey God all his life, and he brought peace and security to his people. He did not live to see their betrayal by his son. Like him, we do what we can to bring the Lord into all the situations of our lives, and trust him for the outcome.

MK

Command and consequence

When God began creating the heavens and the earth, the earth was at first a shapeless chaotic mass, with the Spirit of God brooding over the dark vapours. Then God said, 'Let there be light.' And light appeared. And God was pleased with it and divided the light from the darkness.

The next two weeks of readings are going to concentrate on the subject of obedience. I can hear you groan and begin to dredge up in your mind all the thoughts that this word is associated with, that imply obligation, 'ought', duty and perhaps resentment, rebellion and lack of incentive. That is our fallen humanity rising to the surface in a 'knee-jerk' reaction. Something we need to understand before we see how 'obedience' impinges on us ourselves is the built-in existence of obedience in creation itself.

In the beginning of things, God created the world. When he spoke and said, 'Let there be…' the only possible outcome was that the thing commanded into being came into being. There was no alternative: his word was and is the ultimate command.

We have lost our understanding of the magnitude of the power of God and his word. When we consider it, how can we puny individuals stand in the presence of the Almighty God, whose word can create a universe at a stroke, and say, 'I won't. I don't want to. Why should I?' We have no power or authority of our own and should not be surprised to discover that!

Almighty God, when I sit and contemplate who you really are and the power that there is in a single word of yours, I am amazed that my fallen nature has the gall to dare not to do or to become anything that you ask without hesitation or question. Change my being and my understanding so that I instinctively know what you want of me and for me, and when it is you who is speaking. Help me to respond with trust and love rather than with doubt and hesitation. Amen

AS

Disobedience and mercy

Yes, Adam's sin brought punishment to all, but Christ's righteousness makes men right with God, so that they can live. Adam caused many to be sinners because he disobeyed God, and Christ caused many to be made acceptable to God because he obeyed.

If God had created us without free will, then obedience would not be an issue. Like the universe when it was created, we would respond to his word without hesitation. But God did create us with free will. It was free will that allowed the serpent successfully to tempt Adam and Eve in the Garden of Eden (Genesis 2:15—3:24). God had told them not to eat of the fruit of the tree of knowledge, but they disobeyed God and ate.

That act of disobedience spawned the myriad other acts of disobedience that have occurred throughout history, from the slightest demur to the most horrific acts of violence. Disobedience became an integral part of our being, our fallen human nature. Some people would say that this original act of disobedience affected and defined not only humankind's relationship with God, but also the balance of nature. They would contend that this is why creation itself does not remain within its preordained boundaries and this is why disasters and disease occur.

In today's passage we read that despite the disobedience of one man, Adam, the obedience of Christ in his death on the cross allowed God to redefine our relationship with him. We now have the opportunity to put things right with God and live in obedience towards him. In taking our punishment for us, Christ gives us a fresh start, if we are willing to make the decision to accept it. Obedience does not, however, then become an automatic feature of our new life in Christ; it is something that we have to work at every moment of every day. Obedience becomes an ongoing, active choice born out of a new and loving relationship with the living God.

Meditate on the words, 'Your Kingdom come, your will be done on earth as it is in heaven.' Turn your thoughts into prayer.

                                                                    AS

Obedience and law

If you will only listen and obey the commandments of the Lord your God that I am giving you today, he will make you the head and not the tail, and you shall always have the upper hand. But each of these blessings depends on your not turning aside in any way from the laws I have given you; and you must never worship other gods.

At the very end of yesterday's Bible passage (if you read it in its entirety), we were told that God gave the Ten Commandments so that everyone could see the extent of their failure to obey God's laws (Romans 5:20). The Ten Commandments are the original ground rules (the old 'covenant', which means 'promise') that were supposed to help a disobedient people live in a way that pleased God. Today's passage (Deuteronomy 28) shows us that obedience brought blessing and disobedience brought punishment and curse. The Law was a very onerous system to live under; there was no mercy and no freedom to fail and try again!

In Romans 5:20–21 we discover that because of Jesus' sacrifice for our sins, we can now experience his abounding grace forgiving us, which is God's new covenant, or promise. This doesn't mean that the Ten Commandments are no longer relevant; they are still God's ground rules and we must try, in his strength, to obey them. What the 'new promise' in Christ means is that if we fail, we do not need to experience curse and condemnation, but we can experience kindness and forgiveness—the Father heart of God (Romans 5:21).

Take some time to look at the Ten Commandments (Exodus 20:1–21). Read them through and consider how difficult it is to live up to them and the ways in which we fail to obey God through them. If you need to pray for forgiveness, grace to change and the Holy Spirit's strength to persevere, do that now. Spend some time thanking God the Father that through Jesus we can experience mercy, forgiveness and freedom.

AS

Obedience and love

Jesus said, 'If you love me, obey me; and I will ask the Father and he will give you another Comforter, and he will never leave you… The one who obeys me is the one who loves me; and because he loves me, my Father will love him; and I will too, and I will reveal myself to him.'

For the person who has chosen to follow Christ, obedience springs out of love for the Saviour, not out of the fear of failure and punishment. Many people live under obedience more of necessity than of love, and are often discontented and complaining. If we obey the call of Christ in our lives out of anything other than love for him, we put ourselves back under 'law' and do not live by grace.

Many people find it hard to obey God out of pure love because they have not fully understood that in Christ they are now adopted into God's family. As part of God's family, we do not have to behave like household slaves any more, but can live as beloved children. We no longer need to earn the Father's love; it is freely given to us through Jesus. There is no need to walk in obedience for any other reason than that we are living in a loving relationship with our heavenly Father.

It can be easy to slip back into 'doing what we know we should' because we start trying to earn the right to salvation again, or because God and other people are watching, or because 'it is expected'. When we let this happen we 'sell our birthright' for something much less than second best. Every day we need to ask the Holy Spirit to keep our perspectives in line with God's. We are beloved children, not slaves, and our actions should be motivated as such.

Lord, give me a new and complete understanding of what it means to be loved as your child. May my obedience to you stem from this understanding of love rather than from any erroneous source. Amen
AS

Obedience and listening

Don't ever forget that it is better to listen much… and remember, it is a message to obey, not just to listen to. So don't fool yourselves. For if a person just listens and doesn't obey, he is like a man looking at his face in a mirror. As soon as he walks away, he can't see himself any more or remember what he looks like. But if anyone keeps looking steadily into God's law for free men, he will not only remember it but he will do what it says, and God will greatly bless him in everything he does.

'Obedience' comes from the Latin verb *obedire*, which shares its root with the verb 'to hear' (*audire*). To obey really means to hear and then act upon what we have heard—to see that listening achieves its aim (Esther de Waal, *Seeking God*, Fount, 1984). For the follower of Jesus, listening, hearing and obeying are intimately entwined and should all spring from humility and love for the Saviour.

When I talk to my children, it can be quite exasperating. I have to say what is needed three or four times and even then my words may not get a response! There are three problems: first, I am not catching their attention before I speak; second, when I do speak, perhaps they are not expecting it because they are preoccupied and are off dreaming in their own little world; third, when I get their attention and they have heard me, they don't always do what is asked because they don't like it, don't want to, or can't be bothered!

I know that we are the same with our heavenly Father. We don't expect him to speak, and when he does, we don't hear; and when God does get us to hear, we don't want to obey because we lack the love, submission and humility necessary.

Lord, let every fibre of my being be attentive each moment of the day, expecting to hear your voice. When I hear you, make me humble enough to listen and willing enough to obey. Amen

AS

Obedience and action

Jesus said, 'A man with two sons told the older boy, "Son, go out and work on the farm today." "I won't," he answered, but later he changed his mind and went. Then the father told the youngest, "You go!" and he said, "Yes, sir, I will." But he didn't. Which of the two was obeying his father?' They replied, 'The first, of course!'

These two sons definitely heard what their father was asking them to do, but they both gave very different answers and then did the opposite of what they had said! Jesus says that we are very blessed if we not only hear his words, but obey them (Luke 11:28). It is not acceptable to say, 'Yes, Lord,' and then fail to turn consent into action.

When we find that our response to the Lord is like the younger son's, we must examine our hearts and ask the Lord to remove whatever is stopping us doing what we have said we will do. When our spirit is willing, but the flesh weak, we need the discipline and strength of the Holy Spirit to help us to do what is required of us. Occasionally this can mean rearranging our whole lifestyle so that our priorities permit and facilitate willing obedience. That is quite a challenge.

Most often, we are like the older son: we are honest enough to admit we don't want to do what is required, but after a little while, when we have had time for prayerful reconsideration, we do it anyway. In this situation we need to take care that our actions do not become motivated by the guilt of not wanting to obey in the first instance, but more from our love for the Saviour and our remorse over our selfishness.

Lord, help me not only to be listening for your voice but to want to do your will from the moment of asking. If I am hesitant and unwilling, help me not to be so proud that I can't stop and think again and respond with a repentant and loving heart. Amen

AS

Obedience and submission

Your attitude should be the kind that was shown us by Jesus Christ, who though he was God, did not demand and cling to his rights as God, but laid aside his mighty power and glory, taking the disguise of a slave and becoming like men. He humbled himself further, going so far as actually to die a criminal's death on a cross.

Doing what we know we should, rather than doing what we want, demands humility and submission from us. We were set the ultimate example by Jesus himself, who humbled himself to become a man, and 'became obedient unto death'. Because Jesus knew what it was to be human, he faced the same struggles that we face. We see this especially in the garden of Gethsemane, where he *struggled* to reach a place of acceptance and to say, 'Your will be done', because he knew it would be a difficult and painful path that would cost him everything.

However, none of us will ever know the depth and intensity of struggle that Jesus did because none of us has so much to lose; we are mere humans, not God himself. But if the Son of God was willing to renounce his rights as God, who are we to think that we have any greater right to hold on to our 'rights'? He understands our struggle and is constantly beside us to strengthen and help us when decisions become difficult; but his love demands our humility, commands our submission and graciously waits for our obedient actions.

Humility is the understanding of who we are before God; submission is the acknowledgment of that understanding, which then leaves us no alternative but to obey, to act, in response to the undeserved love of God we have received in Jesus.

'Nowhere you will find rest except in humble obedience… but if God is to dwell among us, we must yield our opinions for the sake of peace.'
THOMAS À KEMPIS

Lord, teach me to recognize when I must yield my opinions for the sake of your kingdom. Amen

AS

Obedience and suffering

Even though Jesus was God's Son, he had to learn from experience what it was like to obey, when obeying meant suffering. It was after he had proved himself perfect in this experience that Jesus became the giver of eternal salvation to all those who obey him.

If we desire to follow the example of Jesus, we must learn to obey his word and his will, but we may need to learn to suffer as a result of that obedience. It is easy to be obedient when it doesn't cost us much and we have to sacrifice little or nothing in the process. We can then easily become a little proud about what obedient followers of Christ we are! The test comes when obedience starts to hurt. Obedience can earn us the criticism of people we consider friends; it can cause misunderstandings at work or in our children's schools. It could cost us our job, our home, our professional reputation.

In the Western world, we don't have much experience of obedience causing us agonizing physical suffering and death, or the loss of family members and the trauma that causes, but many Christians have to face these challenges every single day. Is our relationship with Jesus such that we could endure these things for his sake?

My mind often turns to think about the incident in which an American teenager was shot by a classmate because she was obedient enough to her love of Jesus to stand up and say, 'Yes!' when the gun-wielding youth asked, 'Does anyone here believe in Jesus?' What would we have done in that situation? I would probably have been hiding with the rest of the class.

What is the hardest thing the Lord has ever asked you to do? Why was it so difficult? In retrospect, what would have made it easier to obey? Would you handle the situation differently if you faced it again?

'Let us ask God that he be pleased to give us the help of his grace for anything which our nature finds hardly possible.'
ST BENEDICT

AS

41

Obedience and 'sacrifice'

'Has the Lord as much pleasure in your burnt offerings and sacrifices as in your obedience? Obedience is far better than sacrifice. He is much more interested in your listening to him than in your offering the fat of rams to him. For rebellion is as bad as the sin of witchcraft, and stubbornness is as bad as worshipping idols.'

God had told King Saul to destroy the whole Amalekite nation, its goods and its livestock (v. 3). But Saul, afraid of his own people (v. 24), allowed his men to keep anything that appealed to them (v. 9) and only destroyed what was worthless. He tried to excuse what he had done by telling the prophet Samuel that the animals were for a sacrifice to the Lord (v. 15). God was not convinced, and Saul was rejected as king of Israel (v. 26).

We also try to cut corners with God to make life easier on ourselves while trying to retain an excusable semblance of 'holiness'. We make outward 'sacrifices', but we are inwardly disobedient. When the Lord asks us to do something, we must do exactly what he says, not construct an interpretation of the situation that makes things look nicely religious while working to our advantage. King Saul chose compromise, dishonesty and whitewashed it with excuses and outward religious observances. As a result he lost his kingdom and everything the Lord had planned for him. He set in motion a future chain of events that almost caused the death of his nation in exile. Haman, a descendant of the spared Amalekite king, was the man who, as vengeance for the acts of Saul, plotted to exterminate the Jews in the book of Esther.

If we compromise and side-step like King Saul, we will lose the blessings that God has planned for us, and could cause hindrances to the advance of the kingdom of God without realizing it.

Search me, O God, and know my heart; test my thoughts. Point out anything in me that makes you sad, and lead me along the path of everlasting life. Amen (Psalm 139:23–24)

AS

Obedience to church leadership

Obey your spiritual leaders and be willing to do what they say. For their work is to watch over your souls, and God will judge them on how well they do this. Give them reason to report joyfully about you to the Lord and not with sorrow, for then you will suffer for it too.

One thing we struggle with is obedience to one another and obedience to those who have a spiritual responsibility for us. Submission to others is not considered an important spiritual discipline these days. We are encouraged by secular thought to do what we want and not be influenced by others. This can make the role of Christian leaders onerous. It is difficult to lead a group of people who each think God is calling the church in the direction that suits their opinions! It can be difficult to catch the vision of the church leadership. But part of our calling as followers of Christ is to learn to submit to each other in love and that includes submitting to responsible leadership. Initially we may have to 'force' ourselves to accept something that we struggle with. Eventually our free will bends naturally towards Christ and we become collaborators with him in our willing submission.

Blind obedience is not the same as submission. Critical facilities are neither wrong nor irrelevant, especially in an age where many have experienced the 'spiritual abuse' of those in leadership. Sometimes we need to be reassured that the leaders the Lord has placed over us are doing their utmost to discern the will of God on our behalf as individuals and a community. In these situations we must feel free to ask with the right attitude, rather than murmuring among ourselves and stirring up unsettling emotions in others. Any leaders worth their salt are ready to listen to those they are leading.

'It is an excellent thing to live under obedience to a superior... be ready to consider the views of others. If your opinion is sound, and you forego it for the love of God and follow that of another, you will win great merit.'
THOMAS À KEMPIS

AS

Obedience and parenthood

Children, obey your parents; this is the right thing to do because God has placed them in authority over you. Honour your father and mother. This is the first of God's Ten Commandments that ends with a promise. And this is the promise: if you honour your father and mother, yours will be a long life full of blessing. And now a word to you parents. Don't keep scolding and nagging your children, making them angry and resentful. Rather bring them up with the loving discipline the Lord himself approves, with suggestions and godly advice.

The issue of obedience within the family is a contentious one, especially if we have close relations who don't follow Jesus. The Bible is clear that children should learn to obey their parents. This lays the foundation for them to learn how to submit lovingly and willingly to God and those who will be in leadership over them when they are responsible for themselves and their own family.

We must be clear that our children's obedience can only be expected and nurtured if we bring them up in the loving discipline of the Lord, not making unreasonable demands or expecting them to do things that are beyond God's laws. There should also be room for all parties to learn to be able to ask for and receive forgiveness when things go wrong. Unlike our heavenly Father, we often make parenting mistakes! For the partner of a non-Christian spouse, and for those with unbelieving parents, it may be difficult to discern the line beyond which submission becomes unreasonable, and what sort of response to make in that situation. When disagreements become inevitable, respectful behaviour and a godly life speak louder than angry words (1 Peter 3:1–2).

Lord, teach us to be loving and respectful to our parents and to our children. Show us how caring for each other can break the cycle of selfishness in ourselves and in our relationships. May the obedience we teach them not be for anyone's selfish gain, but for the benefit of the whole family's growth in the love of God. Amen

AS

Obedience to secular authority

For the Lord's sake, obey every law of the government: those of the king as head of state, and those of the king's officers, for he has sent them to punish all who do wrong, and to honour those who do right. It is God's will that your good lives should silence those who foolishly condemn the Gospel without knowing what it can do for them, having never experienced its power. You are free from the law, but that doesn't mean you are free to do wrong. Live as those who are free to do only God's will at all times.

The Bible tells us that there is no government anywhere that God has not permitted to be in power (Romans 13:1–7), so if we rebel against the laws of the land we are rebelling against God. This can be difficult to understand if a country is ruled by an occupying power, especially when that power is used to abuse human rights (but that is not the issue under consideration here). In the time of Jesus, Israel was occupied by the Romans but Jesus still said that the Jews should 'Give to Caesar what is Caesar's' when he was challenged about whether tax should be paid to the Roman authorities (Matthew 22:21). We need to do what is right and pay what is due, so that the name of the Lord is not brought into disrepute.

Lord, help us to see beyond the boundaries of our own small concerns and understand that our system of government is in power only by your concession. When it is difficult to understand 'injustices' in the system, help us discern if our indignation is a product of our selfish nature or rather your concern for people's well-being speaking in our hearts. Teach us to be as obedient as our conscience permits, laying our conscience open to your scrutiny and direction. May we be open to the possibility that you might want to use us as agents of change, at least by increasing our burden to pray about international politics. Amen

AS

When is it OK not to obey?

The administrators... tried to find grounds for charges against Daniel in his conduct of government affairs, but they were unable to do so. They could find no corruption in him... Finally these men said, 'We will never find any basis for charges against this man Daniel unless it has something to do with the law of his God.'

Unless we find ourselves living under a regime which is flagrantly breaching human rights for its own political end, the most usual situation in which we might be unable to obey those in authority over us is if we are asked to do something which is obviously wrong in relation to our walk with God.

Western society has become so multi-faith and politically correct that everyone and anything can be accommodated except the 'established Christian faith' that is perceived to have dominated national belief and way of life for decades. So much so, that the committed follower of Jesus can find it difficult to gain the understanding of secular authorities in relation to their beliefs. In the light of this 'open atmosphere' the lack of tolerance to the practising Christian seems totally illogical. Many Christians believe this is a conspiracy by the powers of darkness to make belief in Jesus unacceptable at all levels of society without anyone noticing the changing tide. It is important that we resist this rising tide.

I withdrew one of our children from nursery school because the school could not understand why their project on Hallowe'en and supernatural darkness was inconsistent with our faith. They would have removed the witch's grotto for anyone else except a Christian! As our society becomes increasingly inclusive, we will find more situations where it is difficult to comply. My example is small, but others struggle with Sunday employment, deliberate corporate mismanagement, and other situations that affect their family's livelihood (Matthew 10:17–23).

Lord Jesus, in the difficult situations that we face for your sake, give us your Holy Spirit to think for us and speak through us, for your name's sake. Amen.

AS

Obedience and reward

*I know you well; you aren't strong, but you have tried to obey
and have not denied my name. Therefore I have opened a door
to you that no one can shut. Note this: I will force those
supporting the causes of Satan while claiming to be mine to
fall at your feet and acknowledge that you are the ones I love.
Because you have patiently obeyed me despite the
persecution… Hold tightly to the little strength you have—
so that no one will take away your crown.*

These verses speak with compassion and understanding about
our human condition. We are not strong, but we try to obey even
when it is a struggle first to discover what it is he wants us to do
and then to find the strength and determination to do it. Often
we pay a great cost for our obedience and risk the possibility of
persecution from others, including our own family. However, the
reward is that Jesus opens a door for us that no earthly or spiritual power can shut. We are welcomed into the Father heart of
God, and his eternal kingdom, now and in eternity.

Despite the costs and the difficulties, Jesus encourages us to
keep on going in the strength of his Holy Spirit, so that we don't
lose our crown. Even when we do fail and wander away from
what he has planned for us, God the Father is still standing at
the open door, like the father in the parable waiting for his wan-
dering child to return. All he demands is our humble obedience,
the step-by-step submission of our will to the will of God, driven
by our love for Jesus, and a daily choice to take up our cross and
follow him so that we can eventually live in his presence for ever.

*I am always thinking of the Lord; and because he is so near, I never
need to stumble or fall. You will not leave me… You have let me
experience the joys of life and the exquisite pleasures of your own
eternal presence (Psalm 16:8, 10a, 11).*

AS

Sharing in suffering

Join with me in suffering for the gospel.

Amar, from Sri Lanka, came into our church at eleven years old, with his mother and younger sister, as a result of a tragic road accident involving the whole family in which his father was killed. Amar became a Christian at a young age and has gone on to greater understanding and deeper commitment as God has been at work in his life. Now, as a young adult, he has taken on responsibilities in the church. There are few things more encouraging to us as Christians than to see young people come to faith in Christ and grow to spiritual maturity and Christian leadership.

Timothy, a young man whom the apostle Paul addresses as 'my beloved child' (v. 2) is just such a 'person of sincere faith' (v. 5). Although naturally shy (v. 7) and not in very good health (1 Timothy 5:23), Timothy is a leader in the church at Ephesus (1 Timothy 1:3). Although Paul has been instrumental in Timothy's conversion and subsequent spiritual growth, and although Timothy had a godly mother and grandmother (v. 5), it is clear from these introductory verses that it is God who has made him what he is.

We may not all be leaders but, if we belong to Jesus, we are all called to be his witnesses. We too need to heed the words Paul addresses to Timothy: 'Do not be ashamed, then, of the testimony about our Lord… but join with me in suffering for the gospel, relying on the power of God' (v. 8). I am sure that this timid young man to whom Paul is writing did not relish any more than we do the thought of suffering. And yet, if we are going to be Christ's witnesses, we will inevitably invite opposition. This is when we must remember—as Paul reminds Timothy—that 'God did not give us a spirit of cowardice, but rather a spirit of power and of love and of self-discipline' (v. 7).

Lord, thank you that I can count on your power as I witness to those around me.

BA

Suffering or shame?

For this gospel I was appointed a herald and an apostle and a teacher, and for this reason I suffer as I do. But I am not ashamed, for I know the one in whom I have put my trust and I am sure that he is able to guard until that day what I have entrusted to him.

'Isn't God supposed to make me happy?' asked Theresa, voicing a question which is perhaps at the back of many people's minds. But nowhere do the scriptures imply that the Christian life is a bed of roses. Sure, the Bible talks of joy, peace, hope, eternal life. All these are ours in Christ. But the Bible never hides the fact that Christians will suffer for their faith. Suffering is one of the themes running through this second letter of Paul to Timothy. Yesterday we saw how Paul exhorted Timothy to 'join with him in suffering for the gospel' (1:8). As a Christian, I must be prepared to meet mockery, misunderstanding, persecution. The apostle Paul knew he was heading for martyrdom because of this gospel he proclaimed. This is the last of his letters. In it he exhorts Timothy to 'guard the good treasure (the gospel) entrusted to [him]' (v. 14) and not to 'be ashamed' of it (v. 8), just as Paul himself is 'not ashamed' (v. 12).

'All who are in Asia have turned away from me,' exclaims Paul (v. 15). In such a world of apostasy and unbelief, Timothy is to continue faithfully to spread the good news of Jesus Christ. Is our world any different? Are we ashamed of the gospel in the face of opposition? Or can we affirm, as did the apostle Paul in his letter to the Christians in Rome, 'I am not ashamed of the gospel; it is the power of God for salvation to everyone who has faith' (Romans 1:16)?

I consider that the sufferings of this present time are not worth comparing with the glory about to be revealed to us. (Romans 8:18)

BA

Suffering like a soldier

Share in suffering like a good soldier of Christ Jesus. No one serving in the army gets entangled in everyday affairs; the soldier's aim is to please the enlisting officer.

This description of a 'good soldier' is the first of three metaphors (together with those of the athlete and the farmer) used by the apostle Paul to describe the Christian life. It speaks to us of single-mindedness, dedication, discipline. A soldier separates himself from civilian pursuits and 'everyday affairs' to concentrate entirely on army matters. Writing this letter to Timothy from prison in Rome, Paul must have had plenty of time to observe the Roman soldiers. He uses them as an illustration to encourage Timothy to be similarly committed to the Lord.

Once again the apostle Paul picks up on the theme of suffering: 'Share in suffering like a good soldier of Jesus Christ.' The kind of suffering he seems to be referring to here is that of self-denial—leaving aside all that would be incompatible with Christian service. This may mean giving up perfectly legitimate pursuits if they take up all our time, thought and energy. It could even cost us our job.

Some years ago, Jim, a member of our church, gave up a good position in a multi-national company in Geneva because he was expected to act in a way that was not possible for him as a Christian. With a wife and four children to support, Jim's decision was not made lightly. But he made the sacrifice because he wanted to follow Jesus wholeheartedly.

Just as the soldier's aim is to please the enlisting officer, so the Christian's aim is to please his Lord and master, Jesus Christ. This means a life of total commitment and dedication to him.

Lord, please show me anything in my life that is not pleasing to you. Help me to renounce all that is unhelpful to my Christian witness and service. May I be willing to 'share in suffering like a good soldier of Christ Jesus.'

BA

Suffering like a sportsman

In the case of an athlete, no one is crowned without competing according to the rules.

This picture of the athlete is not an isolated one in scripture. Several times in the New Testament the Christian life is depicted as a race. The writer of the letter to the Hebrews encourages us to 'run with perseverance the race that is set before us' (Hebrews 12:1). In order to do that, he says we must shed any superfluous weight and entanglements and fix our eyes on Jesus.

In his first letter to the Corinthians, the apostle Paul writes, 'Do you not know that in a race the runners all compete, but only one receives the prize? Run in such a way that you may win it. Athletes exercise self-control in all things; they do it to receive a perishable wreath, but we an imperishable one. So I do not run aimlessly... but I punish my body and enslave it, so that after proclaiming to others I myself should not be disqualified' (1 Corinthians 9:24–27).

And here in our passage today Paul makes it clear to Timothy that, in order to receive the wreath, or the crown, the athlete must 'compete according to the rules'. In order to receive our reward in heaven, the Christian who is saved by grace must live this life in a way that is consistent with the teaching of God's word. For the athlete, as for the soldier, and for each one of us, this means obedience, discipline and commitment.

How perfectly satisfying that Paul is able to say while in prison at the end of his life, knowing that he is soon to die, 'I have finished the race... From now on there is reserved for me the crown of righteousness, which the Lord, the righteous judge, will give me on that day' (2 Timothy 4:7–8).

Let us determine to follow Paul's teaching and example and 'compete according to the rules' so that we too can look forward to that 'crown of righteousness'.

BA

Suffering like a sower

It is the farmer who does the work who ought to have the first share of the crops.

When our children were young, we spent some of the happiest family holidays I can remember on a farm in Somerset. Although our family was living at a relaxed pace for that short time, we were conscious that all around us work was going on as usual. And farmers work hard! They spend long hours in the fields, ploughing, sowing and later tending their crops, often in adverse weather conditions. After such devoted toil, the farmer deserves the first share of the harvest.

How do we apply this picture of the farmer to the Christian life? Paul could be implying that just as the hardworking farmer never has time off—farming is his *life*—so the Christian's faith affects all that he is and does.

But to what do we liken the harvest? We might get some help from another of Paul's letters where he uses a similar illustration: 'Whoever ploughs should plough in hope and whoever threshes should thresh in hope of a share in the crop. If we have sown spiritual good among you, is it too much if we reap your material benefits?' (1 Corinthians 9:10–11). So Paul may have meant that Timothy should expect some kind of payment for his labours.

He may also have been thinking in terms of a spiritual harvest. Timothy's faithful, diligent instruction would bear fruit in terms of spiritual maturity in the lives of those among whom he had worked so hard. Jesus speaks of another kind of harvest (John 4:35), meaning the salvation of the lost—a harvest of souls. Evangelism too is hard work, requiring an investment of time and energy. But the toil bears fruit in terms of conversions and lives committed to Jesus Christ.

May we be wholehearted and consistent in living for Jesus and serving him.

BA

Suffering for the Saviour

All who want to live a godly life in Christ Jesus will be persecuted.

Jews from Antioch and Iconium went to Lystra and 'won over the crowds. Then they stoned Paul and dragged him out of the city, supposing that he was dead' (Acts 14:19). This is an example of some of the persecution Paul endured in the first century.

Jeyaraj was arrested by the police in Sri Lanka and was imprisoned for nearly fourteen months for no crime he had committed. He experienced the presence and love of God even in the midst of much pain and torture—an example of persecutions endured by believers in Jesus Christ at the end of the twentieth century.

Paul had already written to the Romans, 'Do not be conformed to this world' (Romans 12:2). Here, after painting a picture of a godless society, he exhorts Timothy to make a stand for what he knows to be right and true—even if he stands alone. Just as Paul himself had been persecuted for his faith (vv. 10–11), so Timothy must be prepared to suffer in the same way. And so must we. For society is no different today. People are still 'lovers of themselves, lovers of money… lovers of pleasure' (vv. 2, 4). Opposition may be blatant (vv. 2–4), but it can also be more subtle, with religious overtones, so as to deceive (vv. 5, 13).

We, like Timothy, need to 'continue in what (we) have learned and firmly believed' (v. 14); we must stand firm on the truth of God's word. But, of course, in order to do that, we need to *know* God's word. If we, unlike Timothy, have not been taught the scriptures from a young age, let us determine to study them now, for 'all scripture is inspired by God and is useful for teaching, for reproof, for correction, and for training in righteousness, so that everyone who belongs to God may be proficient, equipped for every good work' (vv. 16–17).

Lord, we pray for those who are suffering because of their faith today. May they have the courage, in the face of opposition and even persecution, to stand firm.

BA

Strengthened through suffering

Endure suffering, do the work of an evangelist, carry out your ministry fully.

'So just don't try to convert me!' was Evelyne's parting shot. A confessed atheist, this French schoolteacher resisted my attempts to share the gospel with her. Now—twenty-five years later—retired, no longer an atheist, but not yet a Christian, she is more willing to listen. I could, however, have given up long ago.

Paul tells Timothy to 'proclaim the message; be persistent whether the time is favourable or unfavourable' (v. 2). This does not mean we are to thrust the gospel down people's throats or bash them over the head with a Bible. We need discernment, sensitivity and respect—as well as love and 'utmost patience' (v. 2)—as we seek ways to communicate the good news of salvation in Jesus Christ.

There are many people with 'itching ears' (v. 3) around today, those who 'turn away from listening to the truth and wander away to myths', as well as 'teachers to suit their desires'—people who will tell them just what they want to hear. A current slogan in one of our local supermarkets is 'Feel good'. Products bought in that shop are supposed to make the customer 'feel good'. This seems to be the criterion in the spiritual realm now, too. We no longer wonder if a particular teaching is *true*, but whether it makes us 'feel good'. How subjective and dangerous! Unlike these other teachers, Timothy is instructed to continue to impart 'sound doctrine' (v. 3).

Let us take note of what the apostle Paul wrote to the church of the Thessalonians: 'Do not despise the words of the prophets, but test everything; hold fast to what is good; abstain from every form of evil' (1 Thessalonians 5:21–22).

BA

Ready to obey

About noon the next day, as they were on their journey and approaching the city, Peter went up on the roof to pray.

The story in Acts 10 is one of the most amazing and significant stories in the whole book. The events that took place were made possible largely because of two prayerful and obedient men: Cornelius and Peter.

Cornelius, a Roman centurion who has been drawn spiritually towards Judaism, is visited by an angel who tells him that his prayers and his generous giving have been pleasing to God. The angel then gives him detailed instructions to go and find Peter in the seaside town of Joppa. Cornelius obeys immediately, and sends two servants and one of his soldiers in search of Peter.

Early the next morning, as the search party is entering Joppa, Peter climbs up on to his roof to begin his prayers. However, he is very hungry and asks his host's servants to prepare him a meal. While the food is being cooked, Peter falls into a trance and has an extraordinary vision. In it, he sees a sheet being let down from heaven, filled with all types of animals, birds and reptiles. Then a voice tells him to eat what is in the sheet. The thought is repulsive and offensive to Peter, because he has always adhered closely to the strict Jewish dietary laws. But the voice declares that what God has cleansed is clean indeed.

As Peter ponders the disturbing vision, the Holy Spirit tells him that there are three men waiting downstairs for him, and that he is to go with them. The next day they all set off back to Cornelius' house.

Neither Peter nor Cornelius knew why they had been asked to undertake their strange errands, but they trusted the one who had asked them—and they obeyed.

Dear Lord, help us to be able to hear and obey you. Please give us the type of faith that prompts us to follow your calling, even when we can't see where it will lead us. Amen

CR

The bombshell!

Then Peter began to speak to them: 'I truly understand that God shows no partiality, but in every nation anyone who fears him and does what is right is acceptable to him.'

Possibly, you and I are Christians today because of the extraordinary encounter between Peter and Cornelius recorded in Acts. Finally, after angelic visitations, visions and journeys, the two men meet. Cornelius starts to worship Peter as if he were a god, but Peter tells him that he is only human too. Then they describe to each other the sequence of events that led to their meeting.

At last, Peter understands the meaning of his vision of the unclean animals being offered to him as clean. He explains to Cornelius that, as a good Jew, he should not visit or associate with Gentiles, but that God is doing something new. From now on, they are to accept that the saving, liberating message of Jesus Christ and the gift of the Holy Spirit are meant for all who believe, even the Gentiles.

It is hard for us to imagine how shocking and radical this development was for the early Church. A large part of the identity of the Jewish people was as a race set apart for God, a holy people. Other ethnic groups were considered unclean and unholy and looked down upon. In the racial melting-pot of our world today, we can't begin to understand quite what an effect God's revelation to Peter would have had.

Happily, Peter responded to what God wanted, even when it flew in the face of tradition. When the Holy Spirit fell on Cornelius and his gathered friends, Peter was entirely convinced that God accepted everyone, irrespective of race or previous creed. He ordered those present to be baptized and welcomed them into the small, but growing, body of Christ.

Dear Lord, please help me to put your will above what I may be accustomed to. Show me and all your children how we are to live and how large your heart is for all you have made. Amen

CR

Walls or doors?

*'And I remembered the word of the Lord, how he had said,
"John baptized with water, but you will be baptized with the
Holy Spirit." If then God gave them the same gift that he gave
us when we believed in the Lord Jesus Christ, who was I that I
could hinder God?'*

If only we could all respond to difficult decisions the way Peter did!
He was obedient to God and open and honest with his friends.
Peter returned to Jerusalem, where he was immediately pounced
upon by his fellow believers. How dare he mix with non-Jews?
What did he think he was doing spending time with the unclean?

Peter explained all the stages and amazing events that had led
to Cornelius and the other Gentiles being baptized. He told how,
when the Holy Spirit fell on the unlikely gathering, he remembered the words of Jesus, and realized that he did not want to
stand in God's way.

Peter could have stood between the Gentiles and their full
acceptance into the body of Christ. Instead, he opened the way
for the glory, generosity and grace of God to be made known to
the Gentiles. Sometimes I fear that if it had been some of the present church authorities instead of Peter, they might have wanted
Cornelius and Co. to jump through a few more hoops. They
might have insisted that they could be baptized only after a full
meeting of all the other 'proper' and original believers. They
might even have suggested that a working party look into the
whole issue of the 'irregular' reception of the Holy Spirit and the
possible consequences for the church.

Thank God for Peter! But remember, Peter had experienced
the unwarranted and unexpected love and forgiveness of Christ.
He would never forget how the risen Lord had mended his
broken heart and shattered dreams, even though he had been
entirely undeserving. No wonder God chose Peter for this special
development: Peter could see the Holy Spirit at work and was not
about to stand in the way of his Lord.

Dear Lord, forgive me when I try to limit and control you. Amen

CR

The disciples get a new name

Then Barnabas went to Tarsus to look for Saul, and when he had found him, he brought him to Antioch. So it was that for an entire year they were guests of the church and taught a great many people, and it was in Antioch that the disciples were first called 'Christians'.

The second half of Acts 11 breaks off from Peter's experiences, and picks up the thread of what happened to some of the other believers in the wake of Stephen's stoning.

Some of the scattered disciples still spoke only to the Jews, but others spoke freely to the Greeks as well about the good news of Jesus Christ. The then capital of Syria was Antioch, the third most important city in the world after Rome and Alexandria, and a strong group of believers, both Jewish and Greek, became established in Antioch.

Barnabas was sent from Jerusalem to visit Antioch, and while there he brought many more people to faith. In fact, so receptive and alive was the church at Antioch that Barnabas went off to find Paul to bring him back as his assistant to help minister to the growing numbers of believers. Barnabas and Paul stayed in Antioch for a whole year, teaching and preaching, and the church became Paul's headquarters for his future journeys. It was also in Antioch that the nickname 'Christians', meaning 'Christ's ones', was first used by Gentiles outside the church. No doubt the word 'Christian' was initially used more to insult and tease than as a term of respect, but we know that within a scant generation it had become the common name for those who believed in Jesus Christ. How amazing to think that today there are Christians in most countries around the world. We may bemoan the dwindling congregations in our country, but, happily, there are places in the world where the church is growing as fast as it did in the first century!

Think about how you first heard of Jesus, and what it would have been like to be in the first generation of believers.

                                                                    CR

Disciples launch disaster aid!

The disciples determined that according to their ability, each would send relief to the believers living in Judea; this they did, sending it to the elders by Barnabas and Saul.

I'm sure most of us can remember Band Aid and Live Aid, and some of the other high-profile enterprises aiming to get badly needed food and supplies to people in dire circumstances. More recently, we have heard of the extreme suffering of people in the Balkans, and the continuing plight of hundreds of thousands of refugees, whether from famine, flood or war.

Alas, natural and human-made disasters are not new, but nor is a generous response on the part of Christians. While Barnabas and Paul were still ministering in Antioch, some prophets came from Jerusalem and predicted a severe famine. The church held a collection for the believers in Judea, and Barnabas and Paul were sent to deliver the relief fund in person. This activity was carried out without the benefit of television, radio, daily newspapers, credit cards, cheque books or the Internet. In fact, the Christians at Antioch had no proof that a famine really was going to happen: all they relied on was the word of a prophet. We, on the other hand, can see all too clearly and frequently the appalling suffering that so many people are experiencing today.

As Christians, I believe our response should be threefold. First, we must continue to pray and work for justice, peace and the end of poverty; second, we must respond as generously as possible when disaster does strike, and support all the organizations who do the work on the ground; and third, we should celebrate the peace, stability and prosperity we have, and discover new ways of seeing God's beauty and joy in the midst of times of trouble. Above all, we must become like Christ for others, and extend God's love to those who come to us for help.

Dear Lord, help me to see the needs of my sisters and brothers and to respond the way you want me to. Amen

Read John 10:10.

CR

Remember James

About that time King Herod laid violent hands upon some who belonged to the church. He had James, the brother of John, killed with the sword.

In just one brief sentence, the death of one of the apostles is recorded. James and his brother John had been the second set of brothers called—the first being Andrew and Peter—all of them fishermen. James' father was named Zebedee, and their mother, Salome, may have been a sister of Mary. If that were the case, then James and John would have been Jesus' cousins.

At times, James, John and Peter seemed to form an inner circle of Jesus' closest friends from among the apostles. The three men are recorded as being at the home of Jairus (Mark 5:37), on the mount of transfiguration (Mark 9:2), and in the garden of Gethsemane (Mark 14:33). Jesus gave James and John the nickname of '*Boanerges*', meaning 'Sons of Thunder'. This may have had something to do with the brothers' character and temperament! Luke records that they once asked Jesus whether they should call down fire on a Samaritan village (Luke 9:51–56), and they certainly had a high opinion of their own worth: both they and their mother asked Jesus if they could be seated on either side of him when he entered his glory.

This picture of James makes him sound bold and brash and fearless, but we know that he, along with the other apostles, deserted Jesus in the garden of Gethsemane, and allowed Jesus to be handed over to the authorities. Even James ran away when the chips were down, but after the Holy Spirit had been poured out on the disciples at Pentecost, James found new strength and power to minister in the name of Jesus. At the end, when his own life was threatened, he remained loyal, and accepted death rather than betray his friend and Lord.

Dear Jesus, thank you for the apostles and all they did to spread your message to a world that sometimes refused to listen. Help us to carry on your work in the power of the Holy Spirit. Amen

CR

A way of escape

*Suddenly an angel of the Lord appeared and a light shone in
the cell. He tapped Peter on the side and woke him, saying,
'Get up quickly.' And the chains fell off his wrists.*

Yesterday the focus was on James, and about how Herod had him
put to death. Today the focus is back on Peter. Herod had him
arrested but, because it was Passover, Peter was kept in prison.
After Passover, Herod was planning to stage a public trial in
order to get Peter sentenced to death.

Not only was Peter chained, he was also being guarded around
the clock by four groups of soldiers with four soldiers in each
group. There was no way, humanly speaking, that Peter had a
chance. Then God stepped into the situation in a supernatural
way.

In the middle of the night, an angel appeared in Peter's cell
and, miraculously, the chains fell off Peter's wrists. The angel
then led Peter past all the guards until he was safely outside the
city gate. It was only then that Peter realized for certain that he
was not dreaming! Immediately he ran to a friend's house to let
them know he was free, and then he went to hide out in a secret
location.

Herod was furious and ordered that Peter be found and
brought back to prison. But Peter had vanished, and so, instead
of killing Peter, Herod had all the guards killed.

I honestly don't know why God allowed James to be killed,
and yet saved Peter, but I do know that, ultimately, all our lives
are in God's hands. I do not believe that God decides whose lives
to interfere with, and whose lives to let unfold, but I do believe
that God loves all of us, and has purposes that we cannot fathom.
I also believe that through prayer we come close to the heart of
God, which is where, eventually, we will live for ever.

*Lord, help us to trust in your continual love for us, no matter what.
Amen*

                                                              CR

Give God the glory

On an appointed day Herod put on his royal robes, took his seat on the platform, and delivered a public address to them. The people kept shouting, 'The voice of a god, and not of a mortal!'

I know we're not meant to rejoice at someone else's downfall, but I can't help but feel a surge of delight when I read about how Herod met his end. Very foolishly, he accepted the accolades of his people, and allowed them to call him a god. Shortly after, Herod was struck down, eaten by worms and he died.

However, it is not Herod that I want to focus on today; it is the people who idolized him. Even if Herod had delivered the most impressive speech of all time, it was wrong for those listening to call him a god. We may not call our leaders gods, but I suspect we sometimes place them on very high pedestals, only to see them come tumbling down, or worse still, only to tear them down ourselves when they fail to meet our unrealistically high standards.

Should we expect perfection from our clergy and other leaders, or should we just expect them to point to the way we should all try to live?

I believe that there has only ever been one person who always acted and lived as he taught, and who was never a hypocrite; and that was Jesus. I think the rest of us may try (and some try harder than others) to behave at all times with integrity and consistency, but sooner or later we all fail. Perhaps it would be healthier for us and our leaders if we looked only to God for perfection, and realized that even the finest of people are not perfect—and should never be allowed or made to feel as if they are.

Dear Lord, forgive us for letting other people take your place in our lives. Help us to support and pray for all those in positions of leadership, and help them to keep their feet on the ground and their eyes fixed on you. Amen

Read Exodus 20:1–6.

CR

Being called

While they were serving the Lord and fasting, the Holy Spirit said to them, 'Set apart for me Barnabas and Saul for the work to which I have called them.'

I wonder whether you have ever felt the call of the Lord in your life? If so, how did you respond? If not, do you think you would even know what a call felt like?

Perhaps you see your marriage or your family as a call. Perhaps you are in a job or career that you know is exactly where the Lord wants you to be. Maybe you sense that a certain friendship or way of life is a call for you. Someone once said that the person who is called is the one who can endure. Being called to a particular work, ministry or lifestyle usually gives people a purpose and motivation that keeps them focused and faithful in a special way.

Before I had met my future husband, and before I had any idea that I would be moving to England, I experienced two calls. One was to preaching, and that call came at the age of seventeen! The other call came out of a vision given to me that I would be working in some way with women in leadership. I even forgot about that second call for a long time, but eventually it resurfaced when I was ready to pursue it.

I believe that God is calling all of us, first and foremost, to respond continually to God's love for us. Out of that will come any other, more specific call, if indeed it is to come. If you are not sure that God has called you to anything in particular, do what the early disciples did: pray and fast and then get on with life, and you will probably wake up one morning to realize that God is already using you in a beautiful way!

Dear Lord, thank you for calling each of us to a life held close to you. Forgive us for sometimes losing our faith in you, as well as in ourselves. Amen

Read Jeremiah 29:11–12.

CR

Calling a spade a spade

But Saul, also known as Paul… looked intently at him and said, 'You son of the devil, you enemy of all righteousness, full of all deceit and villainy, will you not stop making crooked the straight paths of the Lord?'

I think most of us find it easier to encourage and affirm people than to tell them that they are out of line. What's even harder is to confront someone who we believe is working against the will of God.

While in Cyprus, Paul discerned that a man who was attempting to pass as a prophet was, in fact, opposing God. One translation has Paul accusing him of trying 'to turn the Lord's truths into lies'. Paul could tell that he was a spiritual imposter, and realized that he was blocking Paul's and Barnabas' ministry. So Paul let him have it!

I have a secret admiration for people who are good at confronting others. I am aware that I often err on the side of giving others the benefit of the doubt, even when there is very little doubt. I'm afraid we have created for ourselves an aspect to the Christian culture that means we rarely challenge or confront—at least to people's faces.

If someone is just irritating or annoying, that's one thing, but if someone is actively working against the Holy Spirit, then that's much more serious, and must not be left unchallenged. Someone once said that all it takes for evil to prosper is for good people to do nothing. If Paul had not exposed the false prophet, the person he was talking to about God would probably not have become a believer. Of course, we must take great care to be sure we are discerning properly, but there are times when we need to challenge those who seem to be actively working against the will of God.

Dear Lord, keep our hearts pure and faithful, and help us to see others as you see them. Please show us when to stay silent and when to speak out. Amen

CR

Know your audience

And we bring you the good news that what God promised to our ancestors he has fulfilled for us, their children, by raising Jesus.

Paul, Barnabas and other Christians left Cyprus and sailed to Antioch, only this Antioch was in Pisidia, not in Syria. On the Sabbath, Paul and his friends went to the synagogue and listened to the Law of Moses being read, as well as some of the writings of the prophets. After that, a message was sent to Paul from the officials in the synagogue, inviting him to speak if he had a word of encouragement for the people.

Paul stood up and began a sermon which outlined the history of the Israelites and traced the judges and kings up to Jesus. Paul spoke about how the other kings rotted in their graves, but that Jesus was different: God had raised him from the dead. What is more, Paul told them, it was only in Jesus that they could have forgiveness of sins, and by believing in Jesus they could be set free from all the sins from which the Law of Moses could never set them free. Paul quoted several times from the scriptures, and in every way demonstrated his deep understanding of the Jewish faith and the history of God's chosen people. Paul was aware that there were also some Gentile converts to Judaism present, and he made occasional references to Gentiles in his sermon. When Paul and Barnabas were leaving the synagogue, the people came up to them and asked them to come back the next Sabbath to explain more about Jesus.

Instead of saying too much, Paul managed to tell the story of what was special about Jesus, and leave his listeners wanting more. What a lesson for anyone who speaks or preaches, or who tries to interest others in the Christian message! The good news that held that mixed congregation spellbound so long ago is as true and relevant today as it ever was.

Dear Lord, thank you for Paul and all those who can communicate about you in a way that is compelling and fresh and lets your truth shine through. Amen

CR

Success breeds... jealousy

The word of the Lord spread throughout that region. But the Jews incited the devout women of high standing and the leading men of the city, and stirred up persecution against Paul and Barnabas, and drove them out of their region.

After their initial positive reception in the synagogue, Paul and Barnabas were invited back. The next week nearly the entire population of Antioch turned out to hear them, but some of the Jewish officials became jealous of them, and immediately began to plot to have them expelled from the city.

If only such incidents were confined to the dim and dusty pages of history, but that is not the case. It seems that jealousy is a human plague that has flourished at all times and that exists inside the Church as much as it does in the rest of society.

We may acknowledge that jealousy is one of the seven deadly sins, but when it strikes, it's awfully hard to get rid of. The best approach is never to let it take hold in the first place, but that is easier said than done. Jealousy gets those who are jealous nowhere; instead, it diminishes them, and it can damage and destroy the object of jealousy.

In Paul and Barnabas' case, they simply brushed the dust of Antioch off their feet and went to another city, but that is not possible for most of us. If we are the ones fighting feelings of jealousy, we need to ask for forgiveness, and resist acting on our jealous feelings. If we are the ones others are jealous of, we must pray for them, and be wise in our dealings with them. Either way round, it might be a positive, healing step to talk to the person or people involved. It is unlikely that we can just walk away from the situation.

Dear Lord, help your children not to be jealous of one another, but if that happens, please help us by the power of your Holy Spirit to face up to it and try to resolve it, for your sake. Amen

CR

Seeing faith in others

In Lystra there was a man sitting who could not use his feet and who had never walked, for he had been crippled from birth. He listened to Paul as he was speaking. And Paul, looking at him intently and seeing that he had faith to be healed, said in a loud voice, 'Stand upright on your feet.' And the man sprang up and began to walk.

As Paul and Barnabas travelled from city to city, they added 'signs and wonders' (Acts 14:3) to their preaching. Some people were convinced that they were of God, and others weren't. They had mixed receptions wherever they went, and the persecutions increased. No matter what they encountered, Paul and Barnabas carried on telling people the good news about the living God.

What impresses me about the story of Paul healing the man lame from birth is that Paul saw and responded to the man's faith. It was the man's own faith that prompted Paul to command him to stand up. This incident is similar to the times Jesus healed people and then told them that it was their faith that had made them well.

I believe and know that God can heal, but I wonder whether I am often enough on the lookout for those who want to be healed and who have the faith to be healed. If being able to give a healing touch to someone is as much, if not more, to do with their faith as it is to do with mine, then perhaps I should be more concerned with looking for open and ready hearts and spirits, and less concerned with how full of faith I might be feeling.

Even though performing miracles and healings had got him into trouble before, Paul didn't hesitate to extend God's healing power to the lame man. Paul's confidence in his Lord was much stronger than any fears for his own safety.

Loving God who longs to make us whole, please help us to see faith in others, and then help us to give to them the touch of your transforming love. Amen

CR

Building the body of Christ

They strengthened the souls of the disciples and encouraged them to continue in the faith.

I once heard the preacher Tony Campolo say that if we spent as much time encouraging each other as we do criticizing each other, what a wonderful difference it would make! In addition to preaching and healing, Paul and Barnabas spent much of their journeys simply encouraging the new Christians and strengthening their churches and fellowships.

I wonder what would happen to our churches if we declared a moratorium on fault-finding and griping, and instead looked for opportunities to tell people all the good things they were doing. In the middle of mindless childhood squabbles, I can remember my mother saying to me and my sister and brother, 'If you can't think of anything nice to say, then say nothing!' What a lot of aggravation could be spared if we still applied that rule to ourselves.

I think we forget how good it feels to receive a compliment or encouraging comment. When people write to me about something I have said in a 'Thought for the Day' or another broadcast, it makes me feel supported and valued. In fact, a kind word can make me glow inside for quite some time.

Of course, there is a time and place for commenting on and trying to correct the negative, but most people respond better to the carrot than the stick. A simple word of encouragement costs nothing, and yet it can make the world of difference. Once, when my children were toddlers, and grizzling during an over-long shopping excursion, a woman walking past me on the pavement caught my eye and gave me a look full of understanding, empathy, tenderness and solidarity. I have never forgotten it. Just one look, and I no longer felt embarrassed, hassled and depressed. I was able to be gentle and loving, which calmed my children, but, perhaps most strangely, I didn't feel alone any more.

Dear Lord, thank you for encouraging us through others. Please help us to make opportunities for building people up instead of tearing them down. Amen

CR

King of glory at the door

Lift up your heads, O you gates; be lifted up, you ancient doors, that the King of glory may come in. Who is this King of glory? The Lord strong and mighty, the Lord mighty in battle. Who is he, this King of glory? The Lord Almighty—he is the King of glory.

I remember watching on television the May Day parades in Moscow's vast Red Square, with their fearful demonstrations of Communist military might—tanks, thousands of massed soldiers and screaming jets flying overhead. I have also looked on at the pomp and circumstance of British state occasions—the Queen in her gilded coach, resplendent in royal robes and crown, attended by courtiers and guardsmen; grand celebrations of colour, music and grandeur before cheering crowds.

But processions like these resemble tiny parties of ants ambling along in the dust compared with how it was when the Lord Jesus ascended and passed through the everlasting gates of heaven after his resurrection! Besides his appearance being dazzlingly majestic, Christ's entry through those 'ancient doors' (previously shut because of sin) signified that he had made it possible for all who trust in his redeeming death to follow him to heaven themselves one day.

One of the amazing truths about our God is that while he is so big, he is also involved in our smallest human concerns. His love encompasses and empowers the entire universe and yet in tenderness he entreats us to open the gates and doors of our lives to him. Jesus is no gatecrasher; he responds when we invite him in humility and faith to be Lord of our lives. Each time we seek him, the door to our inner selves that has been left 'on the latch' is pushed open once more as the Lord comes in.

I see you at the gate of my life, hear you through the door of my mind, feel you on the threshold of my heart. Come, Lord Jesus, King of glory. Redeem me, dwell in me, transform me. Amen

CB

Watching over me

But the eyes of the Lord are on those who fear him, on those whose hope is in his unfailing love, to deliver them from death and keep them alive in famine. We wait in hope for the Lord; he is our help and our shield.

It is said that the eyes are the windows of the soul, revealing a person's true quality and nature. I wonder what the eyes of Jesus were like—as he wept with Mary and Martha at their brother Lazarus' death, when from the cross he entrusted John with his mother, the times he hugged little children, blessing them, or as he challenged the self-righteous Pharisees' hypocrisy? The expressions in his eyes must have vividly reflected his thoughts and feelings.

Psalm 33 revels in God's creativity and power. The one who breathed stars into existence and contained vast oceans in his storehouses also has plans for the people he made. He watches all the time, seeing visible things and the hidden secrets of our hearts. And he responds to what he sees in perfect truth and justice. Revelation 1:14 says Christ's eyes will be 'like blazing fire' when he comes to judge the sin of the world, a fearful sight to all who have rejected him. But the Bible also tells us that the Lord, 'full of unfailing love', longs to rescue us from sin and helps and strengthens all who look to him in faith and hope.

It takes courage to make 'eye contact' with God. He sees right through us, revealing things we may prefer to forget. But if we come humbly before him, that divine 'unfailing love' will be present to forgive, heal and bless us.

Lord, if it were not for the cross I couldn't lift my eyes to you, for you are holy. And you couldn't look upon me because of my sinfulness. But because Jesus came, I can gaze upon your beauty, your face shining upon me in love and grace. May nothing then come between us. Amen

CB

The light of his face

It was not by their sword that they won the land, nor did their arm bring them victory; it was your right hand, your arm, and the light of your face, for you loved them.

This psalm was obviously written at a period of tremendous difficulty and trial for Israel. Enemies were constantly attacking, plundering their possessions and mocking their faith in Jehovah, their rescuer. Things seemed so hopeless that it felt as if God had turned his back on his people, refusing to respond to their prayers for protection and help.

We have all experienced times when everything seems pitted against us, even God himself. However much we pray, confessing all our failures and weaknesses, begging God to help us understand and to keep us going in the darkness, there is only silence. It is a lonely place to be.

God is the same yesterday, today and for ever. 'The Father of the heavenly lights, who does not change like shifting shadows' (James 1:17) never gets into a bad mood, or forgets us or decides not to watch over us any more. Just as the sun shines constantly in space and yet is frequently obscured (especially in this country!), God's promises, his merciful love and his protection continually beam down to us. In his wisdom he sometimes conceals himself, causing us to examine whether we really do trust him even when there is little obvious evidence of his care.

Looking back, the writer reaffirmed God's past faithfulness, reminding Israel that by themselves they would have failed again and again. It's the same for us. 'Without me you can do nothing,' Jesus said. The trial will pass; God is faithful; keep trusting him.

O God, if the sun was not in exactly the right place, we would die. Even shrouded by night or cloud, it sustains us. It is the same with you. Thank you for the strength of your arm in our battles and the light of your face shining on us in love. Amen

CB

Bridegroom

In your majesty ride forth victoriously on behalf of truth, humility and righteousness; let your right hand display awesome deeds... All your robes are fragrant with myrrh and aloes and cassia; from palaces adorned with ivory the music of the strings makes you glad... at your right hand is the royal bride in gold of Ophir.

As a girl I adored stories about handsome princes performing courageous deeds, especially when dragons were involved. The motivation for such bravery was always the promise of marriage to a beautiful princess in dire peril, and they always lived happily ever after. Of course the Bible is no fairytale but there are some interesting similarities in the basic plot.

In our worship and adoration of the Lord, we rightly focus on his death and resurrection, his creative power, grace and glory. This psalm portrays another aspect of Christ as he comes to claim his Bride. The allegory of marriage throughout scripture represents the covenant relationship we have with God, especially in the New Testament. Jesus 'loved the church and gave himself up for her to make her holy... to present her to himself as a radiant church, without stain or wrinkle or any other blemish' (Ephesians 5). Revelation 19 paints a picture of the most splendid wedding ceremony and reception ever—the marriage of the Lamb to his Bride, the whole company of the Church.

Perhaps you are single. Or maybe you married but it has been a disappointment or even failed—nobody's relationship is perfect. Whatever our situation in this life we are certain to find true love in the next. In storybook terms we're the princess and Jesus is the handsome warrior-king who has destroyed all our enemies—Satan, sin and death—because of his great love for us. 'The king is enthralled by your beauty; honour him, for he is your Lord' (v. 11).

My Lord, I want to give you my whole heart, to be closer to you than to anyone else. Forgive me when I draw back or turn away. Thank you for every token of your deep love and faithfulness. Amen

CB

Psalm 71 (NIV)

Confidence from youth to old age

*Since my youth, O God, you have taught me, and to this day
I declare your marvellous deeds. Even when I am old and grey,
do not forsake me, O God, till I declare your power to the next
generation, your might to all who are to come.*

A child I know became a Christian at the age of four, one
evening after his bath. As his mother towelled him dry he asked
her why God had let Jesus die. 'Because Jesus loved us so much
he said he'd take the blame for everything bad any of us has ever
done,' she said. 'You mean Jesus got punished by God because
I'm not good?' the boy enquired in amazement. 'What shall I do?
I'm really sorry.' And so it was that, with tears in his eyes, not
even stopping to put on his pyjamas, he prayed and entered the
Kingdom of heaven. Six years later his faith is growing and he
vividly remembers that moment.

That mother had become a Christian herself as a teenager.
Hugging her son, she recalled the ways that God had led her
through the years. In times of crisis he had given her the wisdom
and courage she needed; he had heard the deepest prayers of her
heart, and there had been so very much to praise him for.

Each generation is indebted to the one before and must pass
on as much as possible to the one to come. This woman's father,
who had hardly prayed since 'giving up on God' during his
painful wartime experiences, had died more than ten years
before his grandson's birth. But God had not given up on him;
and in his final days at a Christian hospice he asked Christ to
save him.

In old age or childhood, through trials and joys, he is the
faithful God from one generation to the next.

*Great is thy faithfulness, great is thy faithfulness,
Morning by morning new mercies I see;
All I have needed thy hand hath provided,
Great is thy faithfulness, Lord, unto me.*

W. Runyan and T. Chisholm

CB

Fortress, stronghold, deliverer, shield and refuge

Praise be to the Lord, my Rock, who trains my hands for war, my fingers for battle. He is my loving God and my fortress, my stronghold… in whom I take refuge… O Lord, what is man that you care for him, the son of man that you think of him?

Today's psalm was written by King David, giving thanks and praise to 'the Lord, my rock' that he had finally secured the throne and subdued his opponents. God had intervened on David's behalf but also equipped him to fight for himself. We are privileged to live in a country that has not been threatened by armed conflict for many decades and our hearts go out to other places where thousands are caught up in the turmoil of war, with families having to flee for safety into inhospitable countryside or across their national borders. Whatever the political rights and wrongs of each situation, many whose future is in jeopardy like this feel that they must take up arms and fight. Tragedies multiply with every offensive and the inhumanity and waste of war fill us with horror and a sense of helplessness.

Such events are one very dramatic outworking of what the Bible calls spiritual warfare. Ephesians 6:12 reminds us that 'our struggle is not against flesh and blood, but against… the powers of this dark world and against the spiritual forces of evil in the heavenly realms'. Few of us are likely to find ourselves exposed to actual battlefields with guns and tanks but we must all confront the effects of evil and live with the reality of suffering sometimes. How encouraging, then, to remember that God is our fortress and refuge. And even when we are unaware of the devil's attack in our lives, nothing escapes God's notice, and he will defend us.

O God our Rock, unchanging and impregnable; be with those today who particularly need your shelter from the storms of life. Grant them courage and strength to stand up for truth and goodness. Heal their wounds and give them your peace. Amen

CB

Giving him our praise

Praise him with the sounding of the trumpet... the harp and lyre... tambourine and dancing... the strings and flute... the clash of cymbals... resounding cymbals. Let everything that has breath praise the Lord. Praise the Lord.

Such excitement and creative energy comes across in this final psalm, as if the writer can hardly wait to gather the band together to start praising. In fact, the impatient instruction 'Praise the Lord' comes repeatedly from Psalm 146 onward—an urgent reminder for us to give him genuine, wholehearted praise.

Praising someone can be relatively easy—admiring their actions, feeling grateful for their kindness—and maybe our relationship with God sometimes stays at this level. As a new Christian, a liberated teenager of the late 1960s, 'doing my own thing', I found the concept of worship very strange. 'Why,' I thought, 'should I bow before anyone? I have my pride.' We often sang the song 'He is Lord' (based on Philippians 2:10): 'Every knee shall bow, every tongue confess that Jesus Christ is Lord'. I didn't mind singing that bit but when it came to the second verse, 'He's my Lord', I stayed silent, knowing that I was unwilling to give myself completely. It offended my self-respect and seemed too risky a commitment.

My pastor often said, 'If he's not Lord of all, he's not Lord at all.' I knew he was right. Praise that isn't attended by an attitude of submission and obedience to God is incomplete. As John the Baptist said, 'He must become greater; I must become less' (John 3:30). The Lord understands that our worship will always be imperfect—in our human frailty we all hold things back—and he accepts whatever we offer in sincerity and truth. So whether we are talented instrumentalists, or just ordinary people giving what praise we can, we must do it with all our hearts!

Praise him for his Holy Spirit, his creative power and his unsurpassed acts of grace. Worship the God of glory in heaven, the Lord of all he has made, the Christ of Calvary; Son of man and Son of the highest! Amen

CB

The king's pardon

'You did not give me any water for my feet, but she wet my feet with her tears and wiped them with her hair... You did not put oil on my head, but she has poured perfume on my feet. Therefore I tell you, her many sins have been forgiven, for she loved much.'

Jesus was invited to dinner with Simon the Pharisee, presumably so that he could be caught out and proved to be a fraud. Strangely, during the evening a prostitute was able to make her way into the dining-room. Were his servants inefficient, or had Simon arranged it? What an extraordinary situation—Jesus gently accepting her attentions with dignity while his host looked on.

'Aha!' Simon thought. 'If Jesus was a real prophet, or even just a reasonably observant man, he'd realize this woman was out of the gutter, unclean and despicable.'

'Let's talk about guilt and forgiveness,' said Jesus, reading Simon's self-righteous mind, and he told of two men, both released from their debts, and how the one who had owed the greater sum was much more grateful than the other.

'It reminds me of what happened here tonight. You, Simon, believe you are above reproach, but have shown little respect—let alone love—to me, your invited guest. But this woman has demonstrated her deep sorrow, her heart overflowing with devotion to me. Her many sins are forgiven; she will leave tonight at peace.'

This is the gospel. Everyone is guilty, in desperate need, and yet so few come to God for forgiveness, to be given a new start. The Pharisee considered himself good enough already but the woman, now bitterly regretting her immorality and the suffering it had brought, repented and was forgiven. She knew her life would have to radically change but her conscience was clear in the sight of God.

Lord, I need not keep hold of any sin because you took all wickedness upon yourself at Calvary. Help me today to turn away from wrong and surrender to your grace and forgiveness. Amen

CB

Mixed emotions

'Don't call me Naomi,' she told them. 'Call me Mara, because the Almighty has made my life very bitter. I went away full, but the Lord brought me back empty.' … Godly sorrow brings repentance that leads to salvation and leaves no regret, but worldly sorrow brings death.

Her menfolk dead and nobody left but two foreign daughters-in-law, Naomi could no longer live with her name (which meant 'pleasant') for her life was bitter—'Mara'. Heartbroken, disorientated and wondering why God had allowed so much grief, Naomi experienced many emotions, including feeling guiltily responsible to make things up somehow to her sons' widows. She was disappointed in God and in no mood to turn to him for help, especially as he appeared to be punishing her. In reality, he had provided the incomparable Ruth and a home for them both in Bethlehem.

When things go wrong we try to make sense of everything, wondering whether we ourselves were at all responsible. Sometimes we are, and should ask God to forgive us and free us from guilt. Although the calamities that befell Naomi's family were not her fault, she needed to repent of her bitter thoughts about how the Lord had treated her. Had she continued to complain, building up a wall of resentment, her story would have ended differently. But Naomi set that aside and as God worked out his purposes in the lives of Ruth and Boaz she watched him create wonderful blessings out of the ashes of disaster.

We can choose whether to take Mara's or Naomi's attitude. Whether we know something is our fault and feel guilty about it, or whether we feel like the innocent victims, we can either trust the Lord or give up on him. He understands our anger and pain; we don't have to hide our feelings or deny our uncertainty. Worldly sorrow, the Mara way, only leads to death. Choose life!

Jesus, please receive me as I come to you for forgiveness and healing where life has hurt me and I have hurt others. Let me know the peace of your love. Amen

CB

The rucksack

'Come to me, all you who are weary and burdened, and I will give you rest. Take my yoke upon you and learn from me, for I am gentle and humble in heart, and you will find rest for your souls. For my yoke is easy and my burden is light.'

Our daughter recently undertook her Duke of Edinburgh Bronze Award camping trip and it took great effort to amass all the equipment and pack it correctly. 'Do you need all this stuff?' I asked her, concerned at the weight of her rucksack (she is quite a slight girl). But yes, everything on the list (and several 'just in case' items besides) had to be crammed in. Waving goodbye as she lurched towards the school minibus, I sent up a prayer for the added strength and cheerfulness she'd need.

Emma and her heavy load set me thinking about the emotional burdens many of us cart around each day. I suspect that many women tend to struggle with vague feelings of responsibility and guilt, whereas men focus more on specific areas in their lives. Most of us could write long lists headed 'I ought to…' or 'I feel bad about…', and live with the habit of worrying and blaming ourselves unnecessarily.

The weary but happy wanderer duly returned, soaking wet, blistered and famished. First we relieved her of the rucksack, hugged her and sent her off for a hot bath. Feeling kind, I began to sort out the bag's soggy contents—tent pegs, maps and squashed food mixed up with muddy clothes. Everything needed to be either thrown away or washed.

Jesus invites us to be free of our heavy rucksack and let him replace it with something far lighter and better fitting. What a relief to lose the burdens of false guilt and needless anxiety, allowing the Holy Spirit to select the 'kit' we should carry.

Dear Jesus, please help me to leave my burdens with you—although it is hard to give them up. I want to carry the rucksack you have chosen for me, knowing you will be beside me always. Amen

CB

Abused and accused

'Don't do this wicked thing. What about me? Where could I get rid of my disgrace?' … Tamar put ashes on her head and tore the ornamented robe she was wearing. She put her hand on her head and went away, weeping aloud as she went.

This is the ugly tale of how King David's son Amnon abused his sister Tamar. While she was caring for her supposedly sick brother, he raped her and then callously banished her from his sight. The young woman was traumatized, her whole life ruined because of this gross act. Tamar ended her days alone, 'a desolate woman' (v. 20).

Most cases of abuse, especially when the victim is young, lead to feelings of worthlessness and self-condemnation. Mercifully few of us have suffered as much as Tamar but we all bear scars, big or small, of rejection, injustice and pain; sometimes dating right back to childhood. Whatever the sources of bad experiences, it is vital to face and understand our reactions to them. Perhaps we blame God, feeling anger and disappointment towards him. And how do we regard those who wronged us?

One of the Bible's greatest themes is forgiveness. Jesus said that without it there is no freedom from sin and death, no reconciliation between us and God. We should forgive others as much for our own sake as theirs, although it is sometimes extremely hard and takes a long time. Forgiving someone who has harmed us means we no longer yearn for retribution but leave the situation to God to justly resolve. It doesn't mean having to see them again, or liking them, but we are released from that desire for revenge. I wonder if Tamar ever came to that place through the important stages of expressing her outrage and pain and ceased to blame herself, lonely and unloved though she was?

Lord, thank you that I can be honest with you about my inmost feelings—for you understand them. Grant me wisdom and the courage to forgive those who have caused me pain. Please help me in your mercy. Amen

CB

'Where are your accusers?'

Jesus straightened up and asked her, 'Woman, where are they? Has no one condemned you?' 'No one, sir,' she said. 'Then neither do I condemn you,' Jesus declared. 'Go now and leave your life of sin.'

Every week women visit CARE's Pregnancy Crisis Centres, which are run by Christians up and down the country. Each centre seeks to offer support to everyone who comes for help, explaining the facts in a balanced way and offering Christ-like compassion in whatever way they can. Many women decide to keep their babies, a few choose adoption but others decide to go ahead with the painful prospect of abortion. These women may suffer reactions of guilt and grief afterwards. Rather than attending post-abortion counselling from the clinic that carried out the termination, though, they invariably return to the Christians who showed no condemnation and offered to be there in their time of painful regret.

The volunteers who work at the centres are a shining example of Christ's love but sadly Christians are sometimes quick to disapprove of those who appear to be in trouble as a result of their own wrongdoing. It takes the amazing grace of Jesus to love and accept people as they are and be willing to help them as they face the consequences of their actions.

The woman in today's passage was dragged gleefully before Christ by the religious leaders who, she knew, wanted to stone her to death. She was in a frightening and hopeless situation— guilty no doubt, but who ever knows the whole truth of any situation, and which of us is blameless? Nobody knows what Jesus wrote in the dust for her accusers to read but it completely overturned the situation: they all slunk off, leaving Jesus and the condemned woman alone together. He had dramatically rescued her from attack. And then he forgave her.

Help me not to judge so much as to listen, to condemn so much as to understand, to reject so much as to embrace. And thank you for forgiving me and setting me free. Amen

CB

Forgiving myself

Day after day every priest stands and performs his religious duties; again and again he offers the same sacrifices, which can never take away sins... Since we have confidence to enter the Most Holy Place by the blood of Jesus... let us draw near to God with a sincere heart in full assurance of faith, having our hearts sprinkled to cleanse us from a guilty conscience.

A symptom of guilt is feeling dirty. Shakespeare's Lady Macbeth, who egged on her husband to murder the king, went mad as her conscience forced her to face their evil deed. Sleepwalking, she tried incessantly to wash away the bloodstains she perceived upon her hands—never able to make herself clean. Many people today, some mentally ill, struggle with the tyranny of obsessive behaviour, eating disorders or depression. Others, less badly affected, still struggle with feelings of guilt.

How can people get free from the shame and remorse of their sin? By trying to make up for it with good or sacrificial deeds? Severely punishing themselves? Some try to deaden their conscience altogether. But humanly speaking there is no real escape from this pit of self-reproach except by receiving full forgiveness from Jesus, being washed clean and made new again as we trust and obey him.

The picture of those priests repeatedly offering sacrifices for sin is very sad. We believe in that 'new and living way' that Jesus has opened for us, which cancels out the old rules and regulations. But to be honest there are probably some areas in our lives we still feel must be atoned for ourselves. As we cast our minds back, there may be certain memories of wrongdoing and failure that hit hard and accusingly. How long should we punish ourselves? If Jesus does not condemn us, why should we condemn ourselves?

Not what I feel or do can give me peace with God;
Not all my prayers and sighs and tears can bear my heavy load.
Thy work alone, O Christ, can ease this weight of sin;
Thy blood alone, O Lamb of God, can give me peace within.
H. BONAR

CB

Beauty for ashes

He has sent me to bind up the broken-hearted, to proclaim freedom for the captives and release from darkness for the prisoners… to bestow on them a crown of beauty instead of ashes, the oil of gladness instead of mourning, and a garment of praise instead of a spirit of despair.

These words were written by Isaiah seven hundred years before Christ stood in Nazareth's synagogue proclaiming that it was he who fulfilled them. What promises of comfort, release, healing and life they are!

Isaiah used an anagram in his message: the Messiah would bestow '*pheer*', Isaiah said, for '*epher*'—beauty for ashes. Rearranging the same letters, he spelled out two complete contrasts. That is how the Holy Spirit works through the experiences of our lives: without necessarily removing problems, he transforms the way we can live with them.

This week we have looked at the burden of inappropriate feelings of blame and guilt that so many of us carry around. The antidote is to surrender our cares to Jesus, particularly when we sense the devil is at work—sowing seeds of condemnation about past mistakes, fear of future failure or unease and doubt at this very moment. Remember that the person who matters has completely freed us from guilt and 'works in [us] to will and to act according to his good purpose' (Philippians 2:13).

Let's make a start in this process of throwing out false guilt. Ask God to show you one thing you feel bad about and ask him to free you from it. My anagram skills are pretty pathetic compared with Isaiah (or even Adrian Plass!) but how about exchanging 'false guilt' with 'life's a glut'—the spirit of condemnation in favour of his abundance!

Thank you, Lord, for freedom and forgiveness. Show me where I hold on to guilt and help me to let go. I want to take your yoke upon my shoulders and walk with you by my side. Amen

CB

Wholeness

*May God himself, the God of peace, sanctify you through
and through. May your whole spirit, soul and body be kept
blameless at the coming of our Lord Jesus Christ. The one who
calls you is faithful and he will do it.*

Pick up any magazine or any newspaper supplement and you will
probably find a feature concerned with wholeness. The emphasis
is mostly on physical health and well-being, with advice on exercise, diet and weight. There is usually little recognition of the
importance of the mind, although one recent advertisement
offers total well-being for body, mind and spirit—if you use the
right cosmetics!

The World Health Organization defines health as a state of
complete physical, mental and social well-being. The Old Testament writers went a stage further and included an ethical context
—obedience to God, or righteousness. They never thought primarily in physical terms for they saw the essential unity of body,
mind and spirit. Peace, *shalom*, best describes the state of wholeness. It is more than an absence of stress or war, for its meaning
includes completeness, soundness, prosperity, well-being, holiness
and maturity. The New Testament adds to this a new quality of
life—life abundant which Jesus brings (John 10:10).

Paul closes his first letter to the Thessalonians with a prayer
for their wholeness. In the next two weeks we shall be reflecting
further on what the Bible has to say on this topic. Paul longs for
the believers to be whole; he knows that God desires wholeness
for them, as he does for you and me.

It raises a simple question. While it is right to keep ourselves
as bodily fit as we can, are we giving this a bigger priority than
our spiritual well-being? Are we being too greatly influenced
by a society which is unhealthily preoccupied with the body?
Should we try with God's help today to think as much of our
spiritual as our physical well-being?

*May my whole spirit, soul and body be blameless at the coming of our
Lord Jesus Christ.*

AE

The complete physician

'The Spirit of the Lord is upon me; he has appointed me to preach Good News to the poor; he has sent me to heal the brokenhearted and to announce that captives shall be released and the blind shall see, that the downtrodden shall be freed from their oppressors, and that God is ready to give blessings to all who come to him.'

I recall, long ago in my medical student days, seeing the ward sister look down the long row of beds in the surgical ward and hearing her say, 'There's the appendix sitting up in bed smoking again.' What a picture!

Identifying a patient by his illness, as if he were an appendix and nothing else, is unlikely today, even in jest. There is an increasing interest in holistic medicine. The deeper understanding of the damaging effect that physical illness can have on one's psychological well-being means that now, when you consult your doctor, he or she will assess your state of mind as well as your physical symptoms, and often consider social factors too. Christian doctors will be aware of the spiritual dimension.

In our Bible reading we get a glimpse of Jesus, the complete physician, standing in the synagogue in his home town of Nazareth, quoting from Isaiah, and then adding, 'These scriptures come true today!' He brings good news of sins forgiven and a new life in loving relationship with God, and also promises healing and growing freedom from the ill in human personality that prevents us from enjoying life to the full.

When I go to him with a particular concern, he sees not only the problem but also everything about me, the whole me. His diagnosis is unerring, his treatment perfect. Nothing is outside his expertise. I put myself completely in his hands, follow his instructions and take the treatment he prescribes.

Lord Jesus, you know far better than I do what is my real need today. Please meet me at that point of need.

                                                                        AE

Do you want to be whole?

[At the pool of Bethesda] a great number of disabled people used to lie—the blind, the lame, the paralysed. One who was there had been an invalid for thirty-eight years. When Jesus saw him lying there and learned that he had been there in this condition for a long time, he asked him, 'Do you want to get well?'

I remember reading this passage in the beautiful St Anne's church near the twin pools of Bethesda. Looking down at those bare, deserted pools, I imagined what it must have been like in Jesus' day—noisy, crowded, long rows of disabled people in colonnades around the edge, waiting for the waters to stir, believing that the first into the water afterwards would be healed. A bit like endlessly waiting in a busy hospital out-patients department, looking up expectantly each time a name is called, hoping it might be your turn to see the doctor. We all know that waiting lists can be long but this one beat them all.

Jesus saw him; his turn had come. 'Do you want to get well?' A foolish question? No, Jesus wanted to know if he was prepared for what would follow. His familiar daily routine would be disrupted. He'd need to find a new home, a job. The invalid explained that there was no one to help him to be first into the pool. Jesus saw that his heart's answer was 'yes'. But he didn't need the pool. 'Pick up your mat and walk,' Jesus said. And he did. At once his weak limbs became strong. There was no physiotherapy or lengthy rehabilitation. He stood on his own feet and walked.

Jesus later found him in the temple. 'See, you are well again. Stop sinning or something worse may happen to you.' He was to walk in new paths, the paths of righteousness. Do I really want to be made whole? It might mean radical changes in my life. There are responsibilities that go with being well.

Lord, I want to be whole. Enable me to pick up my mat and walk.

AE

Wounded but whole

Not many of you were wise by human standards; not many were influential; not many were of noble birth. But God chose the foolish... the weak... the lowly... of this world and the despised... and the things that are not... It is because of him you are in Christ Jesus.

This passage takes me back to the leprosy wing at Manorom hospital in Thailand. I wonder what dread picture that conjures up for you—disease, deformity, poverty, rejection, and isolation? My memories are quite different. I always came away from my visits there with my heart cheered and my faith strengthened. It is true that in the world's eyes these patients were despised, 'things that are not'. There was evidence of their physical weakness—disfigured faces, hands, feet. I know how poor they were materially, what sorrow and hardship most had experienced, some abandoned by their own families. Yet there were eyes that held a peace and contentment that belied outward appearances and circumstances. They had found God and knew they were accepted by him and deeply valued. Some even expressed thanks for the leprosy because it was while attending clinics for treatment that they had heard and believed.

With quiet pride, a young woman showed me her delicate embroidery, painstakingly stitched with numb, almost fingerless hands—for me a symbol of God at work in her life, making something beautiful with what was scarred and damaged. Jesus came with salvation and healing—spiritual wholeness. In him they were made whole (see Colossians 2:10).

God turns our values upside down. Of what use are physical health, education, status, wealth, if there is no spiritual life? God chooses the weak and despised and gives them everything of value in Jesus Christ. Are you troubled by something in your life—poor health, financial worries, family concerns, stress at work, unsatisfactory relationships? Are there wounds and scars that continue to disturb you? Learn from the leprosy patients.

Thank you, Lord: you chose me, to make me whole.

AE

What do I lack?

*'All these [commandments] I have kept,' the young man said.
'What do I still lack?' Jesus answered, 'If you want to be
perfect, go, sell your possessions and give to the poor, and you
will have treasure in heaven. Then come, follow me.' When
the young man heard this he went away sad, because he had
great wealth.*

Here was a young man enjoying many privileges, in total contrast to the leprosy patients we thought about yesterday. He had
youth, wealth, ability, and a position of authority. Yet he was
incomplete: there was an emptiness in his life. He was so anxious
to fill it that he put aside his dignity and ran to Jesus and knelt
before him. He was in earnest. 'What must I do to get eternal
life?' he asked. 'Keep the commandments,' said Jesus, listing
those that dealt with human relationships. The confident young
man thought he had kept all those since boyhood and knew
something more was needed.

Jesus saw his genuine desire and loved him. 'Sell up, give
everything away, and help the poor. Money never merits first
place in your life. Leave it all and follow me.' Jesus saw a man
whose obedience to the commandments did not go as far as
parting with his wealth. His completeness would come not by
adding to what he already had but by distributing it.

The young ruler was taken aback. It was the last thing he
expected. He loved his possessions too much to risk giving them
away. He could not bring himself to throw away the advantages
he depended on, even to gain what he most needed. Sadly, he
stifled his longings and missed the great opportunity. Jesus may
not ask us to sell up, although he may, but prescribes for each of
us individually. When we ask for something to enrich our lives
he may start by asking us to sever ourselves from something we
are holding dear.

*Lord Jesus, you see my need. Give me your prescription and enable
me to accept it gladly.*

AE

The forbidden touch

*And a woman was there who had been subject to bleeding for
twelve years, but no one could heal her. She came up behind
[Jesus] and touched the edge of his cloak, and immediately her
bleeding stopped… Then the woman, seeing that she could not
go unnoticed, came trembling and fell at his feet. In the
presence of all the people, she told why she had touched him
and how she had been instantly healed. Then he said to her,
'Daughter, your faith has healed you. Go in peace.'*

As a doctor, I have seen many patients with prolonged bleeding
but none whose symptoms lasted this long. Doctors do not get a
good press here. Luke, the physician, in his Gospel, merely says
that no one could heal her, but Mark tells us she had suffered
under doctors, spent all her money but only got worse. It's not
difficult to imagine the distress and exhaustion her illness caused
and the restriction of activities and social life that followed.
Under Jewish law (Leviticus 15:19–30) the sufferer was ceremo-
nially unclean and forbidden to take any part in temple worship.
As she could communicate this uncleanness by a touch, she had
to avoid all physical contact with others. How demeaning and
isolating! What a miserable existence!

In her desperation she came to Jesus in the only way she
could—surreptitiously—and, with a forbidden touch, put out
her hand to him. Immediately her bleeding stopped. There was
a surge of well-being. She tried to slip away but Jesus stopped her.
'Who touched me?' Jesus wanted not only to stop the bleeding
but also to heal the emotional and psychological hurt of years of
feeling like a non-person, labelled as unclean. Frightened and
embarrassed, she blurted out her story. Before all the people, in
healing affirmation, Jesus addressed her tenderly as daughter and
commended her faith. *The Message* reads, 'Daughter, you took a
risk trusting me and now you're healed and whole. Live well, live
blessed!'

*Today Jesus says to you: 'Daughter, trust me. Be healed. Be whole.
Live well. Live blessed.'*

AE

Mature and complete

Consider it pure joy, my brothers, whenever you face trials of many kinds, because you know that the testing of your faith develops perseverance. Perseverance must finish its work so that you may be mature and complete, not lacking anything.

Something had upset the two-year-old, who was sitting in his high chair screaming, his face red and tear-stained. His missionary father cheerfully encouraged him to praise the Lord, and after a while the child responded to his father's loving tone of voice and calmed down.

These verses reminded me of that incident, for isn't James saying, 'When life is tough, be happy, rejoice'? We want to do just the opposite and, like the child, kick and yell in anger and frustration. 'Why should I be having to go through this?' we complain. James and other New Testament writers, particularly Peter, say, 'Wait, think. What you're going through will be put to good use if you let it. Your faith will be strengthened. God will work through it to grind off the rough edges and make you complete, the person he wants you to be.'

Jesus warned us to be prepared for difficulties and testings. 'In this godless world you will continue to experience difficulties. But take heart! I've conquered the world!' (John 16:33, *The Message*). God doesn't want us to suffer. We suffer because we are part of a sinful world. The athlete learns how to endure more and more strenuous training to strengthen his body for achievement. Learning to respond positively and creatively to life's experiences will help us grow into wholeness. I recommend this prayer by Thomas à Kempis:

Lord, I see I cannot do this by nature—make me able to do it by grace. You know that I am not able to endure very much, and that I am downcast by the slightest difficulty. Grant that for your sake I may come to love and desire any hardship that puts me to the test, for salvation is brought to my soul when I undergo suffering and trouble for you.

AE

Healing power of forgiveness

When a woman who had lived a sinful life in that town learned that Jesus was eating at the Pharisee's house, she brought an alabaster jar of perfume, and as she stood behind him at his feet weeping, she began to wet his feet with her tears. Then she wiped them with her hair, kissed them and poured perfume on them.

This story has always intrigued me—such an extraordinary, over-the-top scene. What overwhelming love motivated her forgiven heart. Probably, she had been a prostitute, used by men, valued only for her body and her sexual favours, her relationships physical and transient. The people of the town looked down on her and avoided her. Her self-esteem must have been negligible.

Jesus changed all that. He accepted her act of love not with embarrassment or rebuke but with praise. He didn't draw away in revulsion or anger or respond inappropriately. He knew that her emotional demonstration came from true love for him, and her awareness of sins forgiven. He commended her for her great love, which contrasted with the attitude of the Pharisee Simon, his host, who, inwardly despising him, gave discourteous, grudging hospitality.

The woman was renewed and healed in spirit. With joy she received forgiveness; the past was wiped away. To be able to show love and to receive love from such a man would have brought enormous emotional healing. What balm to all the hurts of the past it was to be praised for all to hear! Her mind and outlook, her valuation of herself and others, were transformed. No longer was she the dregs. Shame and degradation were replaced by a new worth. Her guilt was cleansed, her conscience clear. Her will was set to follow Jesus and sin no more. 'Go in peace,' Jesus said. With his complete understanding he did and said exactly what was needed for her to be made whole. No wonder she was extravagant in the expression of her love for him.

You are forgiving and good, O Lord, abounding in love to all who call to you. (Psalm 86:5)

                                                                      AE

Present your body

Therefore, I urge you, brothers, in view of God's mercy, to offer your bodies as living sacrifices, holy and pleasing to God—this is your spiritual act of worship.

I remember the first time I heard this verse. I had just become a Christian. One of the senior surgeons was speaking in the Infirmary chapel at a small lunchtime meeting for students. I had noticed the kindness and understanding he had shown to patients, and the deftness and gentleness of his hands as he examined them and as he operated. In addition, I had been impressed by his courtesy to me when I had consulted him about a cut tendon. He was a living example for us and so I listened all the more intently to his eloquent voice as he urged us to 'present your bodies', 'be transformed', because 'this is your spiritual act of worship' ('reasonable service', AV).

I was learning an important lesson—that being a Christian was more than praying to confess my sins and acknowledge my need of a Saviour. God desired a lifetime commitment of my whole being. My faith should be expressed in how I lived. Believing was not something vague, abstract, only in the mind or spirit, just for Sunday and church, but down-to-earth, practical and involving every minute of every day. I should serve him with my body as well as my mind and spirit. All my ordinary mundane tasks were to be offered to him in obedient service as an act of worship.

This means that the details of our life—how we spend our time and money, our leisure, our friendships—all matter to God. This is not stifling but wonderfully liberating and creative, for Christ will work in us to realize the potential he sees, transforming us to become more fully ourselves, making us whole. It will be a lifetime process. 'And whatever you do, whether in word or deed, do it all in the name of the Lord Jesus, giving thanks to God the Father through him' (Colossians 3:17).

Today, by your grace, I will worship you in all I do and say.

AE

A renewed mind

Do not conform any longer to the pattern of this world, but be transformed by the renewing of your mind. Then you will be able to test and approve what God's will is—his good, pleasing and perfect will.

Today we are increasingly concerned to maintain healthy bodies. Not many of us have to worry about getting enough food. We are well informed and careful about what we eat. We recognize the importance of exercise: gyms and fitness classes proliferate. But do we take as much care over what enters our minds, over its maintenance and well-being? Is our mental diet good and wholesome? Do we avoid what is harmful, seeking out that which is good?

'No man is changed till his mind is changed,' wrote Dr W.E. Sangster, a former President of the Methodist Conference. 'It is into our minds that Christ must come if he is to come into our lives. From our minds he will change our character, discipline our will and control our bodies.'

In our reading Paul warns us to be aware of the culture we live in—'the pattern of this world'—which is far removed from God's. We are not to be so well adapted to our present-day society that we fit into it and accept its values without thinking. We are easily influenced. Ask yourself if your standards are set by books, newspapers, television, friends and neighbours or by God's word. Paul says, 'Don't let the world decide how you are going to behave: don't be like the chameleon, which takes its colour from its surroundings.' We are called to think and act differently. As we determine to make God's standard our aim, he will renew our inner selves, our minds, our thoughts, habits, choices, words and actions. From being self-centred, more and more we will be Christ-centred and know the mind of Christ.

Test me, O Lord, and try me, and examine my heart and mind; for your love is ever before me, and I walk continually in your truth (Psalm 26:2–3).

AE

Wholesome thinking

Fix your thoughts on what is true and good and right. Think about things that are pure and lovely; and dwell on the fine, good things in others. Think about all you can praise God for and be glad about.

In these verses Paul encourages us to think positively in order to develop healthy minds. We are to dwell on all that is good—the true, not the false; the lovely, not the ugly; things to praise, not things to complain about. Cultivating a habit of thankfulness and praise is most helpful of all. We might list in our prayers at the end of each day all we have to be glad about. Fixing our thoughts on what we can appreciate in others, rather than what we dislike, will change relationships for the better. If we allow our minds to be occupied with the good that Paul lists, the influence of these thoughts will be seen in what we say and do.

In one of his books, Richard Foster suggests exercises, small daily disciplines, to build up our Christian life. One suggestion is to pray for other motorists in traffic instead of fuming and grumbling. I tried this. I was amazed at the difference it made. I no longer seemed to meet impatient bad drivers—they were all polite and careful! Of course, it may be that I had changed and not the other drivers. However, there's no doubt about the beneficial effect of my changed thinking. Try it yourself for a week and see what happens.

Peter wrote his letters to stimulate his readers to wholesome thinking (2 Peter 3:1). Indeed this is true of all scripture, which God has given to teach, rebuke and train in righteousness (see 2 Timothy 3:16). For wholeness of mind, we need to study God's word, to immerse our minds in it, allowing it to influence all our thinking and so our behaviour.

Set your minds on things above, not on earthly things. For you died, and your life is now hidden with Christ in God (Colossians 3:1).

AE

Growing through our relationships

...to prepare God's people for works of service, so that the body of Christ may be built up until we all reach unity in the faith and in the knowledge of the Son of God and become mature, attaining to the whole measure of the fullness of Christ.

This is a picture of God's people, the Church, as a perfectly functioning healthy body, the body of Christ. Paul explains that different gifts are given to us so that as we all work efficiently together, the body is built up, our own faith grows and we become fully mature adults—whole, like Jesus. 1 Corinthians 12 shows how each part of the body is necessary, even ones that seem insignificant.

We cannot survive alone, or become whole people in isolation. We need one another to grow in faith and maturity. Our lives gain meaning and worth through our interaction with others. Yet it is in this area that we get problems. We don't like the vicar or the music group or someone in our house group. Others of us feel a deficiency in our relationships. We may be afraid of being rejected or despised if we share ourselves and get too close. Some feel emptiness because they've never married, or had children; and others because of the loss of a loved one. In our place in the body of Christ, we can nevertheless be whole.

As part of his body, we each have a role and are valued for who we are. We need no longer look enviously at others, because this confidence strengthens us to respond to them with growing love and appreciation. We will feel with those who suffer disappointment and rejoice in another's happiness. Someone has said that one of the biggest problems in the Church is folk not getting on. A Dutch friend tells how he was sitting under the stars complaining to God about a friend. He heard Jesus say, 'I died for that man.' Such an understanding transforms all relationships.

Lord Jesus, help me to surprise someone today by my loving response.
AE

Damaging weeds

*Be kind and compassionate to one another, forgiving each
other, just as in Christ God forgave you.*

Bodily and emotional healing is intimately linked with forgiveness of sins. Forgiveness is the foremost healing that Jesus brings; the heart of our faith; the reason Jesus died. What joy we know when we are forgiven and cleansed. 'If we confess our sins, he is faithful and just and will forgive us our sins and purify us from all unrighteousness' (1 John 1:9). There is a natural connection between much of our sickness and our spiritual and emotional health. While disease is not a punishment for sin, there is no doubt that not being right with God or our neighbour affects particularly our emotional well-being. I have often seen with patients how this can lead to physical symptoms too.

Jesus emphasized the need for us to forgive as we have been forgiven (see Mark 11:25). We are reminded of this every time we say the Lord's Prayer. We know Peter's question: 'How many times must I forgive?' And the answer: 'Seventy times seven'—that is, never stop forgiving.

David Watson used to say how damaging the weed of resentment with its bitter root can be. Bitter people miss the grace of God. 'The weed killer for this vicious root is forgiveness—gallons and gallons of it.' Doing it is the difficulty. Once I struggled for a whole weekend, arguing with God and myself because I didn't see why I should be the one to forgive. In the end I did it as a matter of will, not feeling; and selfishly, because I didn't want to miss God's blessing. Letting go of the anger and resentment was painful but brought a flood of love and thankfulness to God and love towards the person who, I now saw clearly, had suffered from my wrong feelings. It may be helpful or necessary to talk with a wise friend, especially if the roots of bitterness go deep. We all need to weed regularly.

*Lord, please help me to grow in wholeness by getting rid of every
damaging weed in my life.*

AE

With my whole heart

He answered, 'Love the Lord your God with all your heart and with all your soul and with all your strength and with all your mind,' and, 'Love your neighbour as yourself.' 'You have answered correctly,' Jesus replied. 'Do this and you will live.'

Love God with all that you are. Be totally devoted to him. Love him with passion and determination, with intelligence and muscle, with no holding back. This is the commandment.

How can we do this? How is it possible to love him in this all-encompassing way? He helps us because 'our love for him comes as a result of his loving us first' (1 John 4:19, LB). He loves us not because of anything we are but because of who he is. He accepts us with all our frailties and deficiencies, yet at the same time desires to change us into people who reflect his glory. This lifelong process of healing our whole person begins as we start 'to grasp how wide and long and high and deep is the love of Christ' (Ephesians 3:18). We can never come to the end of its riches and depth. The more we learn about him, the more we love him.

In this verse, we see total commitment. Our whole personality, with spirit, soul and body in harmony, is to be focused on Jesus. We all have to be wholehearted, single-minded, not splintered people wasting our energy with words, actions, thoughts and feeling, all pulling in different ways.

Richard Foster said that living the Christian life is not gritting your teeth but falling in love. When we know a joyful welling up of gratitude and love for Jesus, we want to spend time with him, talk to him, listen to him, learn from him, sing his praises, please him, become like him. Here again, God helps us because he has 'poured out his love into our hearts by the Holy Spirit, whom he has given us' (Romans 5:5).

Lord Jesus, I want to be wholly in love with you.

AE

'I'm listening…'

'Ask, and it will be given you; seek, and you will find; knock, and it will be opened to you.'

Imagine a pilgrim arriving in heaven depressed, poverty-stricken, harassed, fearful, frustrated, ignorant, joyless and unfulfilled. The pathetic soul limps to the foot of Jesus' throne in tears, pouring out all the earth's agony and woes, and listing, in a voice of resentment and bitterness, all the world has thrown at him or her in life, sobbing, 'Why didn't I get what I needed?' Then imagine Jesus, equally tearfully replying, 'But you didn't ask.' There is no such scene as this depicted in scripture and of course Jesus knows our needs even before we recognize what they are ourselves. But just imagine!

What Jesus does command is that we ask, we seek, and we knock. The sky is the limit in terms of his good gifts available to us, but no promise comes without an accompanying command. This servanthood in relationship with Jesus is a partnership, an interaction, and a growing closer to him.

Jesus always encouraged his followers to approach the Father in an open and trusting manner. His coming to earth expresses the powerful God of the Jews as being in close intimacy with his children. No one had to stand on ceremony to approach Jesus: 'like father, like son'.

Not that an open channel between the Father Yahweh and his people was something new. The Old Testament continually encourages a relationship of mercy. But the visual image of Jesus standing in the midst of his disciples saying, 'Look, if you need something, just ask' holds an alluring poignancy which brings God right to our kitchen table and helps us to realize that we don't have to run for the best tablecloth when he knocks at our door.

Dear Jesus, you promise so much. Why can't I receive? Forgive my unbelief, forgive my lack of trust, forgive my laziness in the search. What shall I ask of my Saviour? Lord, show me what I need. Amen
HMcD

Exhausted?

'Come to me, all who labour and are heavy laden, and I will give you rest… for my yoke is easy, and my burden is light.'

When devout Jews spoke of 'yokes' in religious terms, they were talking about the Law of Moses—the same Law which the Pharisees had expanded to include many additional nit-picking details that even a saint or an angel would have found virtually impossible to keep. To the Pharisees, only strict and burdensome obedience to all the precepts of this Law, including their additions, brought peace of mind. 'Rest', to the devout Jew, was a clear conscience regarding religious duty.

Jesus talks about a new order, an obedience to his way—a servanthood to him, not merely to laws. He did not abolish the Law, but fulfilled it (Matthew 5:17). However, he condemned the Pharisees for their attitudes and behaviour (Matthew 23).

When truly in love, obedience does not have to be a burden. 'Peace of mind' is a heart at one with Jesus. 'Resting' in his love is the ultimate remedy for all of this world's frustrations. But sometimes we just get tired. We ask of ourselves more than a human being can achieve in their own strength, pushing ourselves beyond limits of endurance to please people, to please ourselves, to prove something. How much of all this exhaustion did Jesus ask of us? 'Tired?' he says. 'Then come.' He is our rest.

Dear Lord, I scrubbed and polished and cooked and typed and sewed and baby-sat and telephoned and shopped and did business all through today. I was careful not to break one single law of yours. At least I don't think I did. Maybe I should check again. I need to be sure. I must be perfect. Legs, head, heart, all ache with exhaustion, but maybe I let you down somewhere, some way. Oh dear, will I sleep tonight?

Dear child, there is nothing you can do to make me love you more. Sweet dreams! Your Father in heaven.

HMcD

Never absent

'Go therefore and make disciples of all nations, baptizing them in the name of the Father and of the Son and of the Holy Spirit, teaching them to observe all that I have commanded you; and lo, I am with you always, to the close of the age.'

Here are more commands married to a promise. When Jesus gives us the vision of hard jobs to be done, he knows we need reminding that he is present to do them with us. The disciples at this time believed that they were in a era which would be relatively short. The 'age' would close with the reappearance of Jesus to take his place as head of the Kingdom.

Little did they know how long this 'in-between time' before his return would last—long enough, in fact, for you and me to make our entrance on to the earth's stage. Are there not still disciples to be made? People of all nations to be brought into the Church, new generations to nurture and teach in his ways? His work continues to the very end of time itself.

It has been said that loneliness is the greatest disease of this modern era. In Jesus' day his followers looked for him everywhere and wished him to stay after the resurrection. Nowadays many people are adept at ignoring his presence even when he stands right in our midst. Through his body, the Church, Jesus will always be here, bringing us his enablement by the power of the Holy Spirit. He is keeping his promise; have we kept his command to daily 'go'?

Dear Lord, when I feel most alone, remind me that I am not an only child in your family. When I feel most inadequate, remind me that you always supply the necessary tools for the job. When I feel in need of a vision, remind me of your mission statement from two thousand years ago, still to be fully accomplished before your return. Thank you for never leaving your disciples. Stay close to me also, Jesus. It's not over yet! Amen

HMcD

Live for ever

Truly, truly, I say to you, he who hears my word, and believes him who sent me, has eternal life; he does not come into judgment, but has passed from death to life.'

The American dream still has power to tantalize us. It sometimes seems that the entire advertising industry is based upon the happiness myth, and staying young is not just a culture; in some instances it has become an obsession. Do we believe we are going to live on the earth for ever?

Death is now a subject more taboo than sex ever was. Sometimes we experience a wake-up call that jolts us out of denial. That near-fatal accident, the terminal illness of a loved one, the sudden awareness that time is passing us by more quickly than we had realized, and we wonder where we might buy a ticket for our preferred destination. It's not for sale. Jesus issues tickets free of charge. To heed his word, to believe and to follow is entrance qualification enough. Paul called it 'justification by faith' (Galatians 3:11). It means that we can escape, not the procedure of judgment, but the condemnation which should come at verdict time. Jesus is prepared not merely to stand bail for us, but to free us from prison. He has served the sentence for us on the cross.

Already the quest has ended; eternal life is there for the taking. Unfortunately, not everyone is taking. However, it is never too late to accept the gift that Christ offers. Thankfully, it's free!

Dear Lord, promises, promises, they are everywhere—in junk mail, through our letter-box, chattering on our TV screens, lurking in lottery machines and bookies' shops. They accost our bleary eyes on the way to work every day, blazing from hoardings read often enough to be ignored completely. We are promise-weary in a fickle world of advertising and promotional deceit. Lord, to sacrifice your life is going just about as far as any man can go to keep a promise. Thank you Jesus, I believe; help me to prepare for heaven. Amen

HMcD

Come now, Lord

'And when I go and prepare a place for you, I will come again and will take you to myself, that where I am you may be also.'

By the time John was writing his Gospel, the disciples had accepted the fact that Jesus was not returning in person just as hastily as they had hoped he might. All through John's life he must have been watching and waiting for Jesus. How this promise must have sustained him through his imprisonment on the island of Patmos, separated from loved ones and church fellowship.

With what force and power John clung to that promise in his prison cell, turning his faith into the tangible witness of the book of Revelation. What wonderful visions were forthcoming— pictures together that provided a code to send to the young churches without much fear of the civil authorities cracking the code and arresting the followers. All focused on the return of Christ and the ultimate union that he would consummate with his Church.

The disciples had originally misunderstood the comment that Jesus had made to Peter, 'If it is my will that [John] remain until I come, what is that to you' (John 21:22), as meaning that the beloved disciple would not die. In fact Jesus was just saying, 'What if…?' He was politely telling Peter to get on with his allotted task and mind his own business. Sibling jealousy was not to be tolerated amongst God's children.

There is a sense in which Jesus must have returned to that prison cell on Patmos, or John could not have written what he did. The world may not know his returning yet but have we allowed him to return to us in our daily living, bringing all his resurrection power and Lordship to our everyday experiences?

Dear Saviour, thanks for the plans you have for me in heaven, later. Meanwhile, please come again and walk with me through each day. Thanks to your promise, I don't have to wait until eternity to know your enabling power. Let's start now, Jesus. Amen

HMcD

Costly fruit

'I am the vine, you are the branches. He who abides in me,
and I in him, he it is that bears much fruit, for apart from me
you can do nothing.'

Jesus often echoed the Old Testament in his teaching. The imagery of 'the vine' would have been a familiar one to his disciples from many different Old Testament books. However, here they learn that it is not Israel who is the vine, but Jesus himself. Jesus promised us the fulfilment of bearing much fruit, but first we must abide in (be engrafted into) his life and will.

In our era, much emphasis is placed on the individual, especially in the West—human rights, the strengthening of self-esteem, individual need-fulfilment and the reaching of full potential for each individual. It has brought freedom and health to many who were once downtrodden and enslaved. Nevertheless, we must be wary of the temptation to subscribe to the 'cult of the individual' to the extent of a 'me first, last and only' philosophy.

All gardeners appreciate the powerful implication of engrafting one thing on to another. It is not merely attachment, or living as neighbouring plants, but it is sharing the same sap, growing together, becoming an integral part of each other in such a fashion that to separate the original graft is to render it dead. Once the graft has truly 'taken', it has become fully united with the host, and they are one. They share a common lifeblood and produce common fruit. Now the very survival of the branch depends on the strength of the host.

Dear Lord, can we grow closer together? Will it hurt in the pruning? Will the tree-surgeon's tools be sharp and cold? What's that you say? Your Father is the gardener and you are the vine. This gardener I can trust and there is no one I should want to grow more like than you. Please make me what I must be to bear fruit for you. Amen

HMcD

A challenging promise

But he said to me, 'My grace is sufficient for you, for my power is made perfect in weakness.' ... For the sake of Christ, then, I am content with weaknesses, insults, hardships, persecutions, and calamities; for when I am weak, then I am strong.

No one knew what 'weakness' felt like more than Paul. His vulnerability showed in his ongoing struggle with temptation, in his physical disability, in his past failures, in his present persecutions, his lack of preaching ability, his small stature and, upon occasions, his inability to get on with colleagues. Humanly speaking, he also had plenty to 'boast' about: his Roman citizenship, his intellectual prowess, his religious knowledge, his writing abilities, his grasp of theological niceties, his ability to encourage the early churches, his reputation as a leader, his courage in the face of much suffering and imprisonments, his missionary travels for the Lord, and the way he handled natural dangers encountered on the journey—not to mention his revelations from Jesus, and his ability to be sensitive to just what the young church leaders needed when they needed it. And on top of all this, I dare say he made pretty good tents. Well, they had to be good; it was his living.

Yet what does he choose to highlight as one of the most powerful tools in God's hand? His weakness! Not his sin, but his inadequacies. I know what he means. It is on the days when I drag myself out of bed aching all over and dreading what must be tackled that day that I properly cry, to Jesus, 'Lord, I can't do today!' It is on days like these that my Saviour says to me, 'Why don't we do it together, then, Hilary?' It is then that God makes the day possible, not in my strength, but in his.

Saviour, thank you for wasting nothing of my life, not even what I might think of as my weaknesses. Challenge me to recognize your 'grace' provision on a daily basis until I feel your strength in all things. Amen

HMcD

Questions of prayer

*Suppose one of you has a friend, and he goes to him at
midnight and says, 'Friend, lend me three loaves of bread,
because a friend of mine on a journey has come to me, and I
have nothing to set before him.' Then the one inside answers,
'Don't bother me. The door is already locked, and my children
are with me in bed. I can't get up and give you anything.'*

Our church has recently completed a congregation-wide survey
on prayer. The awkward questions ranged from favoured positions, frequency and style to ways in which God communicates
to us—very comprehensive and very challenging. Unfortunately,
I scanned my copy on one of those 'is-God-listening?' days. I had
no idea how I was going to answer the detailed questions. To me,
God felt shut up behind some very formidable doors just then,
and I had no confidence that he would even hear me knocking.

I suspect we all have times when prayer flows naturally and
times when it does not. Some of us try to emulate prayer models
which do not suit us. Sometimes life hurts too much to concentrate. Sometimes we wonder if God is occupied and unavailable,
as in the opening scenario of Jesus' parable. This midnight
request was pushing the boundaries of even Middle Eastern
hospitality, so Jesus knew that the natural sympathies of his
listeners would be with the man closed up for the night.

Is it all too easy to ascribe a similar reluctance to God? When
the compiled results were available from our church survey, I saw
that our approach to prayer is very much that—*our* approach.
We may experience real and often profound frustration in our
stumbling attempts to connect with the Almighty, but God is not
like us. The survey revealed a kaleidoscope of praying practices
and bore witness to a glorious variety of God's responses. Perhaps
if we started more often with *his* agenda and *his* ideas for prayer,
then we could short-circuit our difficulties.

Lord, teach us to pray.

Read Luke 11:1–4.

DA

Pray and pray

I tell you, though he will not get up and give him the bread because he is his friend, yet because of the man's boldness he will get up and give him as much as he needs.

The idea of boldness here carries with it persistence and perseverance. Jesus' hero gets what he wants because he keeps going. He is prepared to risk his friendship by being a bit of a nuisance, but it works. He gets his bread.

All of us have times when we feel inconvenienced by others. I suspect that most of us would try to avoid being the source of inconvenience. It has been said that women are relationship orientated and are perhaps more motivated by this than men. I am sure this is not universally true, but I must admit that my husband finds it impossible to understand why, when I am on the telephone to ask a friend a simple question, I have to find out how the family are, what the news is, how she is feeling and so on. A two-minute phone call is never that! I would have phrased the late-night plea in this parable very carefully.

How does this affect the way we approach God? I wonder. Do we ever catch ourselves checking up on our relationship with him, feeling hesitant, wondering about his response? There's nothing wrong with sorting out things that need it, but Jesus is encouraging boldness and persistence in prayer. What would militate against that in our own personal prayer life? What internal blocks dissuade us from approaching prayer with confidence? Is there anything that, even today, would hold you back from a good talk with your heavenly Father?

We all have our different battles, and perhaps that is why Jesus tells the parable. He knows what God is really like and does not want us to miss out because of our limited understanding. It is OK to be bold. It is OK to expect.

Take the risk of giving prayer some quality time—today.

Read Hebrews 4:14–16.

DA

Prayers and answers

So I say to you: Ask and it will be given to you; seek and you will find; knock and the door will be opened to you.

Right, says Jesus. If persistent knocking on a reluctant friend's door will yet bring results, let us apply that to your prayer. First, can you really imagine God being reluctant? Second, he is more than your best friend. Third, the bread you are after is of a different batch altogether. We are into another league here. We are dealing with a lavish creator God who even knows the number of hairs on your head (Matthew 10:30). We are talking about the sustainer of the universe (Psalm 8), the one who loved the world so much that he gave up his only Son to rescue it (John 3:16). Keep things in perspective.

This is the God who responds to our longing with assurances that it will be met. The contrast between the grudging friend in the parable and our generous God could not be greater. When we stop and consider the vast richness of all he has made, how can we possibly suspect him of stinginess?

We still do, though. Well, I do. I assign to God the same small-mindedness of which I am often guilty, and think he will act accordingly. I suspect he will mete out assistance if he has the time. I need to look again at the words of Jesus and take them at face value. There is no proviso or condition to this sequence: 'Seek and you will find.' I have been encouraged by some friends who have recently become Christians. They have searched and they have found. They did not know God and now they do. The seeking was not easy but they now have a priceless treasure. Wherever we are on our life's journey, the principle is the same. God wants to be found.

Do not be outdone by the man in the parable. Put your heart into it and find what you need.

Read Luke 18:1–8.

DA

Prayer promises

For everyone who asks receives; he who seeks finds; and to him who knocks, the door will be opened.

These are amazing promises. Jesus tells us that the basis to our prayer life is an expectation that we will receive what we ask for. We are to build the foundation for our prayers on this understanding. God will give. He will be found. He will be welcoming. We will get what we are looking for.

However, I do not know how you react to these wonderful promises to prayer, but I venture to suggest a hitch. Why, when it all sounds so simple and glorious, does it not always work? Before you write me off as heretical, let me explain. I quite understand that these promises follow the first utterance of the Lord's Prayer, and that we must see them in context. My husband's not receiving the motorbike he prayed for is not a big theological problem. It was low on the list of priorities for 'your kingdom come', right? But you cannot be a Christian for very long before you hit some big unanswerables on this prayer business. There are things that must surely be within 'your will be done', which refuse to happen. Or happen when we do not want them to. The child who is killed. The loved one who does not respond to God's love. The marriage that breaks down. The war that will not end. The pain. These things seem to fly in the face of receiving all you ask. Indeed we would not ask for them. They open huge debates about the nature of God, the world, the devil and humanity.

Jesus lived in the same world and yet he still insisted that we would find what we long for. He does not leave us pat solutions, but instead invites us to tussle with reality, all the while building on his promises.

Father, give me right foundations and right understandings. Amen

Read 2 Samuel 12:15–23. How do you understand the concept of God's will?

                                                                    DA

Trusting prayer

Which of you fathers, if your son asks for a fish, will give him a snake instead? Or if he asks for an egg, will give him a scorpion?

I have never been to the Holy Land but would dearly love to visit one day to see if my overactive imagination is anywhere near the mark. I want to find out if my picture of Jesus standing near the water, addressing the crowd, could be fitted into a real landscape. This scorpion comment is precisely the sort that sends my mental pictures into overdrive. There is no way that such a ridiculous suggestion would have been met with anything else than laughter, and suddenly there I am, surrounded by ordinary people in unfamiliar garb. The children are running round the back, the cynics are clustered just in front of them, the hurt are squeezing down the side, the curious are all ears… and suddenly a ripple of laughter from all as Jesus reminds them of their common humanity.

Of course they know how to feed their children! How then, implies Jesus, could God know any less? Of course their children, startled from their games into listening, know they can trust their parents for provision. How then can we grown-ups expect any less from our heavenly Father?

Of course we are just like them, in need of reassurance. Jesus' understanding of humanity echoes down the centuries and hits the mark. We too need encouragement to trust God completely for all our needs. We too need his impeccable logic. How could God provide in any less a way than we do? How could he be anything less than the perfect parent? Yet we need to clasp these words close to our souls in the face of a hard world that would tell us they are not true. In the sight of all that would discourage us, we must learn that God is to be trusted and is exactly who he says he is.

You prepare a table before me in the presence of my enemies. You anoint my head with oil; my cup overflows. (Psalm 23:5)

DA

Luke 11:13 (NIV)

Intimate prayer

If you then, though you are evil, know how to give good gifts to your children, how much more will your Father in heaven give the Holy Spirit to those who ask him!

A bit of Gospel comparison here. Nothing too heavy, in case you are reading this first thing in the morning and, like me, it takes you a while to come round. Matthew's Gospel also records the teaching about asking and receiving, but he tells us that God will give us 'good gifts' instead of the Holy Spirit (Matthew 7:11). There was a time when I could easily grasp Matthew's version— everyone can envisage good gifts—but I was not sure about the Holy Spirit. A while and some gentle theology later, I came to appreciate that the Holy Spirit is just about the best good gift you can get.

So when Jesus talks about us receiving the Holy Spirit in answer to our asking, he is promising us more than we can imagine. He is not setting up a slot-machine kind of trust where we drop in the request and God duly pays out. God is looking for relationship. He wants us to experience his love for us, because there is nothing else like it; and he wants us to love him back, because there is nothing to equal that either. Getting our foundations for prayer fairly stable becomes a springboard for a friendship with God that is totally unique to each one of us. The unanswered problems do not disappear, but as we discover that God is totally trustworthy, we can trust him for the things we do not understand.

All of this sounds excellent and to be desired. If you are anything like me, however, there are moments when heaven feels almost tangible and moments when the whole thing feels impossible. Sometimes it is by sheer decision of the will that we come to God at all, and at other times no one can get us away. Prayer is nothing if not interesting.

Keep on going!

Stuck for prayer? Try a psalm.

DA

Secret prayer

'But when you pray, go into your room, close the door and pray to your Father, who is unseen. Then your Father, who sees what is done in secret, will reward you. And when you pray, do not keep on babbling like pagans.'

So, prayer. We have Jesus' own teaching on prayer as a basic inspirational structure; we have parables to encourage us and promises to build on. Over the next few days, we will pick up on different aspects of prayer to which Jesus draws our attention.

If you have ever been discouraged by someone's seeming expertise in prayer, take heart. Jesus has no time for those who prayed to show off. Dare I say that I have occasionally wondered if a particular pray-er was truly addressing God, or rather aiming to impress the rest of us? That sounds judgmental, yet Jesus raised the subject! Prayer is not about flowery language or popular techniques. Prayer is about honesty and relationship. So if you catch yourself longing to spout a few choice phrases at the next prayer meeting, it might be better to keep quiet until you get home. Trying them out alone with God should soon sort out whether they are coming from your heart or your ego. Take a leaf out of Jesus' book. He often withdrew from the crowds to pray alone (for example, Matthew 4:23). He would get up early, or stay behind late. He always prayed before major decisions. I would love to have eavesdropped on his conversations with God. No wonder the disciples were fascinated and asked to be taught to pray. They could see how important and special it was to Jesus.

Different personalities will find different ways of praying appropriately. I am learning not to copy others but to find my own style. Your relationship to God is just yours, so find what is right for you. Gather ideas from others and experiment, then enjoy exploring your unique pattern. Remember that God himself will reward us for our efforts, so go ahead—discover what that means.

DA

Prayer first

Jesus entered the temple area and began driving out those who were buying and selling there. He overturned the tables of the money changers and the benches of those selling doves, and would not allow anyone to carry merchandise through the temple courts. And as he taught them, he said, 'Is it not written: "My house will be called a house of prayer for all nations"? But you have made it a den of robbers.'

Can you imagine the chaos? Mark describes the scene with typical understatement, but this was no polite disagreement. Jesus drove out the merchants—in his version, John tells us he used a self-plaited whip (John 2:15)—and tipped up tables. This outer court of the Gentiles was already a noisy, busy place. Would-be worshippers haggled over the price of a sacrificial dove, merchants touted for business, lambs bleated, money clanked and ordinary folk jostled their way through. Suddenly there is a disturbance near the doors and in strides Jesus, causing mayhem as he flings tables to the floor. Birds fly free of crushed cages, money cascades on to people's feet, sellers escape as he approaches. Why doesn't anyone stop him or question him? Isn't it awesome as he marches through, breathing authority and anger?

The Jewish leaders concluded that he was way out of line, but Jesus' priorities were clear. This was his Father's house. It was built for prayer, not for people's greed and extortion. It was not just the inflated prices for worship necessities, but the human-centred atmosphere that Jesus was objecting to. This temple was a holy place of pilgrimage for all, a place to meet with God.

As the Holy Spirit leads us into a warm and intimate relationship with God, it does not mean we are to treat casually things that he takes seriously. Would we have noticed the mixed-up priorities in the temple that day? Is the challenge to ask God to help us to see things as he sees them?

Would you have supported Jesus' actions?

Read Micah 6:6–8.

DA

Children's prayers

Then little children were brought to Jesus for him to place his hands on them and pray for them. But the disciples rebuked those who brought them. Jesus said, 'Let the little children come to me, and do not hinder them, for the kingdom of heaven belongs to such as these.'

There is no doubt that Jesus' prayer life was something special. It sprang from a unique relationship with God and it made things happen. Small wonder that parents wanted to bring their children to him for prayer. Perhaps the disciples thought the children insignificant—hardly pivotal to the exciting opening up of Jesus' ministry and extraordinary teaching. As usual, Jesus turned human perception on its head. He welcomed the children and gave them quality time. He told off his disciples for getting the wrong end of the stick and declared to all that the children had special access to the kingdom of heaven.

So he set a precedent for us—on the one hand, the obligation to pray for and bless our youngsters; and on the other, actually to strive to be like them. Having taught us to pray for God's kingdom, he now encourages us to approach this kingdom with the dependent, trusting and sincere attitude of a child. Children generally have no choice in being dependent. We grown-ups easily forget that we are dependent too. Yet coming to God on any other basis is illogical, for we are dependent for our every breath on the one who made us. Some of us struggle with the illusion of our independence, and find that it can get in the way of trusting prayer. Watching my daughter climb on to her father's lap for a snuggle reminds me again of the principle. To paraphrase our parable: if earthly fathers can give hugs that well, how much more wonderful can one from our heavenly Father be?

Where were you when I laid the earth's foundation? Tell me, if you understand. (Job 38:4)

Pour out your heart to God, your Father. He understands you better than you do.

DA

Praying for persecutors

But I tell you: Love your enemies and pray for those who persecute you, that you may be sons of your Father in heaven. He causes his sun to rise on the evil and the good, and sends rain on the righteous and the unrighteous.

This has to be one of the most challenging things Jesus ever said. The desire for justice and vengeance seems deeply embedded in humanity, and is surely the prime cause for many of the world's conflicts. The fate of nations turns on the principle of revenge for past wrongs. Jesus challenges us at the deepest level when he commands us to pray for our enemies. I know I am not alone when I react to this with hesitation. 'But Lord, those actions were inexcusable…'; 'But Lord, that was so unfair…'

We all have an inbuilt fairness monitor, biased in our favour. Even for small slights, we struggle to let the perpetrators off the hook. For Jesus to ask us to pray for those who have hurt us, whether in a minor or major way, seems patently unfair. Surely God is a God of justice? Yet Jesus says we must pray for those who have injured us. I think this is incredibly difficult. The hurt is real. The injustice is obvious. To pray for blessing demands that we forgive and release our demands for vengeance. Yet on the few times when I have battled through to obedience on this one, I have discovered—eventually—a remarkable healing for my own sore spirit. Laurens van der Post explains the effect of forgiveness on his fellow confinees in a Japanese prisoner-of-war camp, when they extended it towards their captors:

> *The tables of the spirit would be strangely and promptly turned and we would find ourselves without self-pity of any kind, feeling deeply sorry for the Japanese as if we were the free men and they the prisoners—men held in some profound oubliette of their own minds* (The Night of the New Moon, *Penguin, 1986*).

Is forgiveness a feeling or an action?

Read Matthew 6:14–15.

DA

Fast and pray

The spirit shrieked, convulsed him violently and came out. The boy looked so much like a corpse that many said, 'He's dead.' But Jesus took him by the hand and lifted him to his feet, and he stood up. After Jesus had gone indoors, his disciples asked him privately, 'Why couldn't we drive it out?' He replied, 'This kind can come out only by prayer and fasting.'

OK, so if we take this story at face value, it could seem pretty wild. The boy reacted to Jesus' ministry so dramatically that the onlookers thought he had died. This was not a quiet, subtle prayer moment, it was a major deliverance session. Some of us might find the whole concept of spirit invasion and its subsequent banishment hard to swallow, but Jesus obviously did not. He dealt with the situation quickly and calmly, and reassured his frustrated disciples that they had been up against a tough situation.

Sometimes things are like that. Sometimes it seems we hit a deadlock in a situation, and no matter how hard we pray, it just will not shift. We battle on, but feel up against insuperable odds. Frustration sets in, and we are tempted to get discouraged. Well, we are not alone. The disciples obviously felt the same. They had done everything they could think of, and still the boy was not better. Then along comes Jesus to rescue them.

The disciples would have been used to the concept of fasting (Matthew 6:16), and Jesus clearly expected them to exercise this particular discipline. Here he implies that it released an extra shot of power that was just what was needed. Perhaps fasting is already part of your worship pattern, but if not, I recommend you give it a try. It is not always easy, but it sorts out your priorities immediately. It can clear the channel between you and God for those resistant situations, and focus your attention on what really matters.

Father, teach me your ways. Give me the courage to try something new if you want me to. Amen

DA

Prayer and guidance

Going a little farther, he fell with his face to the ground and prayed, 'My Father, if it is possible, may this cup be taken from me. Yet not as I will, but as you will.'

This moment, of course, took place in the garden of Gethsemane, immediately before Jesus was arrested prior to trial and crucifixion. The Gospels record that Jesus was overwhelmed with sadness, and actually repeated this prayer three times. I cannot help thinking of a couple of hymns that imply that Jesus tripped quite happily into suffering. This was not the case. He was extremely distressed and wanted out. He knew what was coming and hoped for another way.

I find this both encouraging and challenging. Encouraging because it reminds me that Jesus was fully human, and shied away from suffering like the rest of us. Challenging because he submitted fully to the will of God in the face of it. His was the ultimate prayer of surrender.

Often when I pray for guidance, I do have an idea of what I would like the future to be. My family and I have recently moved jobs and location, and I had filled the waiting-for-guidance time with a multitude of possible plans. None of these came to be, and I had quite a struggle letting go of some of my better ideas. I was not in the least ready for God's plan when it came, and felt I was back in the kindergarten of guidance school. Sometimes submitting to God's way is a terrific challenge and throws us back to the basics of trust in his goodness and character. It is heartening to remember that Jesus had the same tussle, despite being God's Son. But in the end, saying 'yes' to God's will has to be the best decision.

'For I know the plans I have for you,' declares the Lord, 'plans to prosper you and not to harm you, plans to give you hope and a future' (Jeremiah 29:11).

How do we trust, in the face of certain suffering, as Jesus did?

DA

Pray and stand

He said to them, 'Pray that you will not fall into temptation.'

Just as Jesus repeated his desperate prayer to God that there might be a way other than the cross, so he also exhorted his disciples at least twice in the garden to pray that they would not fall into temptation. Yet while he was wrestling with deep anguish, his friends had collapsed with exhaustion and sorrow, and were sleeping. It is very easy to condemn the disciples for not standing with Jesus in his hour of need, but would we have done any different? Surely we too would have been confused by Jesus' increasing agitation, and scared by the escalating tension of the night. Besides, he was the strong one: we leaned on him. What did he mean by temptation?

Jesus knew all too well what trials the disciples would face in the ensuing days, and only wanted to prepare his friends. It's interesting that he picked this particular angle on prayer for the days ahead—rather than, say, praying that they would be delivered from evil. The disciples would certainly be hounded and threatened by the authorities, but Jesus' main priority was that they would stand the test and keep their faith.

How often do you pray that you will not fall into temptation, when faced with difficult situations? I must admit that my first prayer is more likely to be, 'Lord, get me out of this!' But Jesus urges us instead to pray that we will not fall—into despair, into discouragement, into hopelessness or lack of faith. He wants us to stand, and not give in to an easy way out if we know it is wrong, or if it will damage others. Sometimes choosing not to listen to temptation is very hard, and we may need the support of a good friend or two. Perhaps that is why we are to pray that we will not fall—before it hits us.

Thank you, Lord, that we can handle this together. Amen

Read Luke 22:31–34.

DA

Jesus, prayer and you

My prayer is not for them alone. I pray also for those who will believe in me through their message, that all of them may be one, Father, just as you are in me and I am in you. May they also be in us so that the world may believe that you have sent me.

If you have never read John's account of Jesus' prayers for his followers before his crucifixion, now is the time. John 17 is so wonderfully reassuring. Jesus prays for himself, his disciples, and then... *us.* He prayed that we also would be caught up into the glorious union that is Father and Son and good news and unity with each other—something so special that it seems hard for Jesus to put it into words.

It is good to know that we were there in that original prayer, when Jesus was entrusting all he really cared about to his Father. Jesus only prayed because he knew the power of prayer and knew that his Father would listen. As we draw our fortnight of focus on prayer to a close, I hope that you have been encouraged. Wherever you are in your prayer experience, keep going, and do not fear to try something new. The trouble with writing these notes is that inevitably I challenge myself, probably more than anyone else. So I will join you in a renewed approach.

In case we still need any more convincing, how about this: university psychologists have published the results of a survey among 474 students which claims that daily prayer wards off depression.

> *We measured depressive symptoms, anxiety and self-esteem and found people who prayed daily or often were more likely to report lower depression, lower anxiety and higher self-esteem than those who hardly ever prayed. They were, however, unable to explain where the power of prayer came from.*
> (The Times, 12 November 1999).

So, now that it is official, how can we resist?

Dear Father, set my prayer life alight by your Spirit. Teach me to pray. Amen

DA

A Saviour foretold

The Lord God said to the serpent… 'I will put enmity between you and the woman, and between your offspring and hers; he will crush your head, and you will strike his heel.'

At first sight these seem strange words, but they lie at the heart of this story.

I don't worry about whether the story of Adam and Eve and their disobedience is historical, or whether it is like a parable, a story that teaches God's truth. Just as we speak about the sons and the father in Jesus' parable of the prodigal son as if they were 'real' people, I speak about Adam and Eve and the serpent as 'real'. We do not throw the 'baby' of God's vital lessons out with the 'bath water' of questions about historicity.

God's generosity, the framework he gives us to live by, the wrong and disobedient choices we often make, the guilt, the attempt to escape from God, the evasion of responsibility, the inevitable consequences—these are real experiences, as up-to-date as when this book was written. It must have been devastating for Adam and Eve to be thrown out of God's beautiful garden, even if they recognized that they deserved it. So what would they make of God's words to the serpent? 'He will crush your head, and you will strike his heel.'

It is wonderful that, in the midst of his disappointment with Adam and Eve, God gives the first hint of a Saviour. That is why this passage is the first reading in a traditional carol service, as we approach Christmas. Satan, the serpent, will continue to make a nuisance of himself to 'the woman's offspring'. ('You will strike his heel.') But the final outcome is certain. 'He will crush your head' is Satan's final, total defeat through Jesus, the woman's descendant; this is one aspect of the triumph of Jesus' death and resurrection.

Thank you, Father, for your promise of a Saviour. Thank you that your righteous judgment and your merciful love go hand in hand.

                                                                    RG

Genesis 22:1–18 (NIV)

The limit of sacrifice

I will surely bless you and make your descendants as numerous as the stars in the sky... Through your offspring all nations on earth will be blessed, because you have obeyed me.

Not everyone reading this is a mother, yet all can imagine the pain Abraham must have felt when the Lord tested him to the limit by asking him to offer his son as a sacrifice. 'What? Sacrifice Isaac, born to us in our old age, after we had waited for decades for a child? Is God asking that of us?' Yet Abraham was willing to obey God and to trust him. He had the knife ready to kill Isaac, who was already tied up and lying on top of the altar, when God called out to stop him. What a relief for Abraham! You can read the story in this chapter.

And what about Isaac? How frightened the boy must have felt. Yet he submitted to it all, trusting his father for what was happening.

'Through your offspring all nations on earth will be blessed.' Here is another look forward to Jesus. We realize that God the Father could identify with Abraham's pain: 'God so loved the world that he gave his one and only Son, that whoever believes in him shall not perish but have eternal life' (John 3:16). God the Son could identify with Isaac's fear: 'My Father, if it is possible, may this cup be taken from me. Yet not as I will, but as you will' (Matthew 26:39). 'My God, my God, why have you forsaken me?' (Matthew 27:46).

While Abraham and Isaac were reprieved at the last minute, for God—Father and Son—there was no sudden halt. Yet the agony of death and separation was the prelude to the glory of the resurrection, that through Abraham's offspring, all nations of the earth might be blessed—you and me included.

Abraham trusted God and obeyed him. Jesus trusted his Father and obeyed him.

Father, please help me to trust and obey you when life is tough, and when it is easy.

RG

Isaiah 11:1–9 (NIV)

Jesus' character foretold

A shoot will come up from the stump of Jesse… The Spirit of the Lord will rest upon him—the Spirit of wisdom and of understanding, the Spirit of counsel and of power, the Spirit of knowledge and of the fear of the Lord.

Adam, Abraham, Jesse. We continue to trace through their descendants to the Messiah. The Old Testament is the first instalment of Jesus' story. Let's see how Isaiah's words, written six centuries before Christ, describe his character.

'The Spirit of the Lord will rest upon him'. Do you remember how, after Jesus' baptism, right at the start of his public ministry, the Holy Spirit was seen to descend on him like a dove?

'The Spirit of wisdom'. His opponents tried to trap him with awkward questions. He always had a wise answer, often in the form of a counter-question that put them in an awkward corner!

'The Spirit of understanding'. The twelve-year-old, taken by his parents to Jerusalem, was found in the temple courts among the theologians, 'listening to them and asking them questions. Everyone who heard him was amazed at his understanding.'

'The Spirit of counsel'. When his disciples deserved rebuke or needed encouragement; when the bereaved widow in Nain, and Lazarus' sisters, were grieving; when the woman discharging blood, and Jairus—so different—were both scared: Jesus' words and manner always showed he understood.

'The Spirit of power'. A storm on the lake; a demonized man; water turned into wine; an invalid of thirty-eight years—just a few of the situations in which his power was exercised.

'The Spirit of knowledge'. Jesus knew just what people were thinking! The grumbling Pharisees, the Samaritan woman at the well, the paralysed man: he knew what was going on inside them all.

'The fear of the Lord', summed up as he said, 'I do always those things that please' my heavenly Father.

Thank you, Jesus, for the same Holy Spirit available for me. Please make me more like you through your Spirit at work in me.

RG

Startling news

Do not be afraid, Mary, you have found favour with God. You will be with child and give birth to a son, and you are to give him the name Jesus. He will be great and will be called the Son of the Most High. The Lord God will give him the throne of his father David.

How would you react if an angel were suddenly to appear in your kitchen, and greet you, 'Highly favoured, the Lord is with you'? Would you feel excited? Amazed? Scared? The story of the angel coming to Mary is so familiar that we can easily overlook the shock she must have felt, first at the angel's presence, then at the enormity of his message.

'You have found favour with God.' What, me? I'm only an ordinary young woman. I'm nobody special.

'You will be with child.' But I'm a virgin. I've not slept with Joseph, or with anyone else. What will the neighbours think? What about the disgrace on my parents?

'You are to give him the name Jesus.' I won't forget that. Jesus—Joshua—he will save. That is special.

'He will be called the Son of the Most High.' Wow! That sounds like a title of divinity. Can this be true? I must pinch myself to know that I'm awake!

'The Lord God will give him the throne of his father David.' But it is six centuries since our people have had a king! King? God? What does all this mean?

Mary was perplexed. But her acceptance is amazing: 'I am the Lord's servant. May it be to me as you have said.' Even if she did not fully understand all that the angel said, something rang true with her. This was genuine. This was of God. It is clear from the Gospels that Mary was no wimp. Yet her submission to this staggering news is an example to us of trust and of obedience.

Lord, I pray that you will give me the resources to enable me to cope with surprising news as equitably and trustingly as Mary did.

RG

My Saviour indeed

'Do not be afraid. I bring you good news of great joy that will be for all people. Today in the town of David a saviour has been born to you; he is Christ the Lord.'

I look back to a carol service fifty years ago, soon after my Christian faith had come alive. I had grown up in a family who often went to church; school had Scripture lessons and chapel services. I was not a questioner; I accepted what I was taught. It was as if a fire had been laid ready, but no match had been applied. It was lit when I discovered how I could invite the Saviour's Spirit into my life.

Then I was asked to read a lesson at the student carol service. The story of the shepherds was very familiar to me. 'Today… a saviour has been born to you.' The words jumped out at me, made fresh impact. A saviour had been born, not just for the shepherds years earlier, but for *me*. Because I, law-abiding on the outside, but impure inside, had recognized that I needed to change. Now I had let that Saviour into my life to be Christ the Lord for me, I could read that lesson with conviction and joy.

The shepherds were terrified at the sudden appearance of the angel. 'Don't be afraid.' They listened; they responded; they went. Some people are scared when they hear the good news about the Saviour. It's good news, but fear of the implications of change in their lives inhibits them, so that they stay in the fields, as it were. But—to change the imagery—a fence is an uncomfortable place to sit! If you have never said, 'Yes, I will go to find the Saviour', why not let this Christmas be the decisive time?

What can I give him, poor as I am?
If I were a shepherd, I would give a lamb.
If I were a wise man, I would do my part.
Yet what can I give him—give my heart.
CHRISTINA ROSSETTI

RG

The real joy of Christmas

*When they saw the star, they were overjoyed. On coming to
the house, they saw the child with his mother Mary, and they
bowed down and worshipped him. Then they opened their
treasures and presented him with gifts of gold and of incense
and of myrrh.*

There could hardly be a greater contrast between the shepherds
and the wise men. The shepherds, local agricultural workers who
lived with their sheep, had been told they would find a saviour.
The wise men, astrologers who came from a distance, and lived
with their books and their charts, were painstakingly searching
for the king whose coming had been indicated by the stars. Yet
they had one great thing in common: they all came to see the
infant Jesus. As Paul wrote, 'There is neither Jew nor Greek,
slave nor free, male nor female, for you are all one in Christ Jesus
(Galatians 3:28). Race, social status, gender: all common ground
when we come to worship Jesus.

The shepherds probably came empty-handed; the Magi came
with gifts—gifts that we can see are symbolic for Christ. There
was gold—for a king; incense—for a god; myrrh—for suffering. I
was deeply moved by a Christmas card that portrayed Jesus'
manger in a room with a window which had one vertical, one
horizontal bar. As the sun shone through the window, the shad-
ow of the cross fell on the manger. The joy of Jesus' birth looked
forward to the pain of his crucifixion.

The wise men understood that this was a stupendous event.
Yet they probably didn't realize the full significance of their gifts.
Two other things stand out from these verses: their joy and their
worship. When we first 'find' Jesus for ourselves, we do not know
all the implications there will be for our lives. But we can come
with joy, and we can begin to discover what it means to worship
him, as we say, 'Jesus, aren't you wonderful!'

*In all the busy-ness of preparations to celebrate Christmas, may I take
time to worship Jesus.*

RG

God's revelation

In the beginning was the Word, and the Word was with God,
and the Word was God. He was with God in the beginning.
Through him all things were made; without him nothing was
made that has been made. In him was life, and that life was
the light of men. The light shines in the darkness, but the
darkness has not understood it.

Unlike the other Gospels, John does not start with stories about
the ancestry and birth of the human Jesus, but with a powerful
declaration of his divinity. Words are for communication. God
sent his Son, the Word, to communicate to us about himself.
That Word came in human flesh, sharing human experiences,
human weakness, even human mortality. It is almost incredible
that he should start his life of human limitation as a helpless
baby, and end it in the vulnerability of a crucified criminal. But
John gives us a glimpse of the glory of his divinity. 'In the beginning was the Word, and the Word was with God, and the Word
was God.' Pause to repeat those words; chew over them; marvel
at them, and at God's eternal, infinite immensity.

'Through him all things were made; without him was not anything made that has been made.' This takes me to the start of the
Bible. 'In the beginning God created the heavens and the earth'
(Genesis 1:1). And Jesus was there, sharing in the creation of the
world. 'The earth was formless and empty; darkness was over the
face of the deep… And God said "Let there be light"'—light to
penetrate the darkness. Sadly, the human beings he put in
charge of his good creation were disobedient; relationships were
spoilt; even creation itself was spoilt. So darkness remained. And
Jesus came as light in the darkness, the 'true light' (v. 9), the
light of which all other lights are but a pale imitation/reflection.

In the middle of all the Christmas preparations, remember the Word—
the infinite God revealed to us in Jesus. And let us allow his light to
shine in the dark corners of our own lives.

RG

Mary's example

And she gave birth to her firstborn son and wrapped him in bands of cloth, and laid him in a manger, because there was no place for them in the inn.

I remember how anxious I was when my children were born. I'd been to classes, had regular check-ups, done my exercises, packed my case (about a month early!) and checked every five minutes that there were no roadworks on the route to the hospital. Mary was young, was in a strange overcrowded town, had been bumped around for days on the back of a donkey, and her mum was miles away. She'd probably been dreaming of a comfortable inn, with a friendly owner giving her a nice cup of tea and a sympathetic hug. Then what happened? Nobody cared. Nobody said, 'Take my room, dear, I can see your need is greater than mine.' Nobody said, 'I can sense that you're having a particularly important baby—sit in this comfortable chair while I make you a meal.' Nobody took any notice of her at all. The best she got—and she was pretty relieved to get even that—was a smelly stable, with used straw and no heating.

In her position I'd have started complaining even before I got to Bethlehem. Why hadn't Joseph had the sense to insist that they set out earlier? Why hadn't he sent ahead to book a room? Why was everybody else having a better time than they were?

And yet I get the feeling from what we know of Mary that she didn't complain; that she just got on with having God's Son as best she could; that she trusted in God to look after her, whatever the difficulties of her circumstances and the problems she was facing. Maybe at this stressful yet glorious time, when family tensions can run pretty high and we can be in danger of forgetting what it's all really about, we too could ask God to help us to stay focused on him, and rejoice uncomplainingly.

Lord, help us to be understanding and forgiving.

WP

Rejoice!

The heavens proclaim his righteousness; and all the peoples behold his glory.

The world was turned upside down. A tiny baby brought God to live down our street, to be the person we could moan to when things went wrong, and the friend who would be delighted when we were happy. A helpless, crying baby, unable to survive for a day without his mother, brought heaven and earth together and gave us a telephone line to our Almighty Creator, which is never off the hook or engaged. This little life transformed the world, gave us the words to ask for forgiveness and the encouragement to start again. Today the whole of creation danced for joy.

I once heard a sermon at a midnight communion, which went something like, 'Jesus has been born this minute for us. Think about it. Alleluia!'

We tend to be a bit immune to all this rejoicing stuff. During the day, maybe we'll attend a fairly traditional service, sing some very familiar carols, open some predictable presents, watch a film on television which we've seen before, eat too much lovely food and do endless amounts of washing-up. By the evening, the stresses of too much excitement for the children, and too many people in the house, may be beginning to show. Or the whole day may feel like an empty shell because the people we wanted to be with us could not be. Christmas is far from an easy time for very many people.

But hang on a minute! These are the trappings that we have laid over the real Christmas—the birth of that tiny baby who changed the world. We should be able to eat a scrambled egg in a prison cell, and still rejoice that today the whole of life turned from black and white into colour. We just need to keep on reminding ourselves not to take the trappings of the day so seriously that we miss the angels singing, and the skies filled with God's glory.

Lord, help us to rejoice!

WP

Anna's example

Anna… [aged] eighty-four… never left the temple but worshipped there with fasting and prayer night and day. At that moment she came, and began to praise God and to speak about the child.

I know a wonderful lady in her mid-eighties, with a wicked sense of humour. Despite using a wheelchair, she is about to travel to a remote monastery on the other side of the world, a journey that would terrify me!

Anna must have been a pretty determined lady too. Most people were maybe a bit afraid of her. To spend your days in prayer wasn't too bad, but your nights as well? And fasting at her age was really taking religion rather more seriously than could possibly be good for her. Couldn't she just have accepted her age gracefully, and taken up knitting instead of going in for all this heavy religious stuff?

But Anna knew what she was doing. She was waiting. She'd had seven years of marriage, then many years on her own, with plenty of time to work out where she wanted to be. And she was right there, hanging on for whatever it was that God was going to show her. She was good at just being, good at praying, strong on patience. When she saw Jesus, she knew what all the waiting had been about. She'd made sure she was in the right place and really tuned in to God.

I suspect that if I had seen baby Jesus, I'd probably have made some inane comment about what nice eyes he had, unaware of who he was. I'm usually too busy rushing about to be tuned in enough to recognize God. We all need to learn to be still, to give God some quality time and to practise the discipline of waiting. If we were half as determined as Anna, God could get through to us, even at this hectic time of year!

Even if it's only for a short while, try to be still and focused on God.
WP

Free gifts

Forgive, and you will be forgiven; give, and it will be given to you. A good measure, pressed down, shaken together, running over will be put into your lap; for the measure you give will be the measure you get back.

This is about the time when I start bargain hunting, using my unerring ability to find something I want drastically reduced in the sales. This, of course, involves the discipline of never buying anything unless it is sale time, and having the ability to convince yourself that dark maroon is really your favourite colour and goes perfectly with the rest of your wardrobe!

Imagine then how a shop would be besieged if it advertised 'Bargains all year round. All genuine customers will be overloaded with free gifts!' If we can be so thrilled with our material bargains, surely we ought to be even more ecstatic about what God & Son (World Suppliers) promise to give us. Free!

There's a catch, though. There always is! We have to be able to receive these free gifts. We have to forgive little James when he breaks the toy we spent so long searching for. We have to be grateful to Aunt Maud when she takes for ever to peel the potatoes, when we could do it so much more quickly if she didn't insist on being helpful. We have to love the family when they seem to think we are the only ones in the house capable of loading and unloading the dishwasher. We have to forgive our friends when they don't phone; forgive our children when they take us for granted; give of ourselves to make others happy.

Is it worth the effort? Well, is it worth having free gifts from God's generous store piled up in our arms? We don't love and value others in order to be rewarded, but God does promise that if we do our best, with his help, then good things will certainly follow.

Lord, help me to see the good in everyone I know.

WP

Joseph's example

*Now after they had left, an angel of the Lord appeared to
Joseph in a dream.*

The wise men had just set off to go home. Mary and Joseph must
have been pretty exhausted, their heads full of the strangeness of
it all, wondering whatever would happen next. In that situation,
if my husband woke me up in the morning and told me that he'd
had a particularly unpleasant dream involving people trying to
kill our baby, I'd have muttered soothing words about under-
standable stress surfacing in dreams. With all the excitement and
worry, nightmares were only to be expected!

But Joseph must have been utterly convinced that this was
for real. To uproot his little family, leave the security of the place
they now knew and rush off into an unknown land must have
taken complete conviction and belief. Joseph knew a message
from God when he heard it.

So Joseph saved Jesus' life. He could have convinced himself
that rational people had outgrown such mystical imaginings.
He could have stayed silent, for fear of looking a fool. He could
have quashed God's promptings, and put the glimmers of the
Almighty firmly to the back of his mind. But he didn't, and God
used this receptive and quick-thinking man to protect the tiny
baby who would turn history upside down.

I wonder how often we ignore the glimpses we get of God? It
may be a very little thing he is prompting us to do—I certainly
doubt if he is wanting us to move to Egypt! But maybe we are
being prompted to forgive someone, or to say sorry ourselves.
Maybe we are being pushed to see something from someone
else's point of view, or to volunteer to take some of the weight
off another's shoulders. Perhaps God is encouraging us to make
time for someone, even perhaps for him. We are all different, but
God can nudge us forward in ways that are just right for us. We
all need to listen to his guidance, as Joseph did.

Lord, help me to listen to your promptings.

                                                              WP

Read between the lines

How much better to get wisdom than gold! To get
understanding is to be chosen rather than silver.

We get lots of letters at Christmas, in which old friends are trying valiantly to sum up their year on one side of A4. At one end of the spectrum could be, 'Gemma (aged ten) has gained a distinction in her Grade 8 piano exam, and is taking her GSCE Maths next summer. My husband Philip is now the company director.' At the other end comes, 'Life continues pretty quietly here, except that Henry's eyesight is a little worse.'

I tend to feel sorry for Henry's family, and think Gemma's are showing off too much! But maybe we should read between the lines, to see a harassed mum struggling to cope with a tremendously gifted child, with no help possible from a husband who is over-busy and pressurized at work.

Sometimes it's easier just to accept the superficial reading of a situation. Perhaps we too are guilty of giving the wrong impression. We can learn from Jesus' approach to people, though. He was very good at the follow-up question, not just stopping at the quick answer. He saw the true nature of people behind their masks, and helped them to see life more clearly. He was tough on hypocrisy but not quick to condemn, seeing the worth of the most unlikely people.

We can ask for his help to see beyond the superficial in all our dealings with people. And when we are given little glimpses into other's lives through their cards at Christmas, perhaps we can seize the opportunities they bring to be in closer touch with the sender, or to pray meaningfully for them. My father-in-law used to keep all his Christmas cards and each day prayed for the senders of five of them in turn, trying to imagine what it was like to be in their shoes. I doubt if they ever knew that a few lines written at Christmas were used to support them all year.

Lord, help us to see with your eyes.

WP

Simeon's blessing

And the child's father and mother were amazed at what was being said about him. Then Simeon blessed them.

Mary and Joseph had a huge task ahead of them. Not only were they new parents, but they knew for certain now that this child was special. They must have wondered if they were up to the task. Everything Jesus learned in his early years was to come from them—they would teach him how to talk, how to behave, how to respect God and value his word. They would protect him, comfort him, encourage him, and then teach him how to stand on his own feet without them. They would lay the foundations of whatever was to come. So Simeon blessed them, giving them God's seal of approval and his promise to help and strengthen them.

Tomorrow we will look forward to a new year, but today let's look back. Who were the people that brought God into our lives, teaching us as Mary and Joseph did Jesus? Maybe our parents first brought God's love to us, or perhaps it was a powerful speaker or a patient friend. Maybe it was someone who had seen us through difficult times, or maybe we read a book whose author spoke directly to us. Take time to think of these people, to thank God for them and to pray for them.

What about the last year? Have certain events helped to teach us something of God? Events both happy and sad, where we felt ourselves swept away by the joy of it all, or carried by a patient Father, comforting his injured child? We could thank God for his presence with us, and pray for situations that are not yet resolved.

And are there people towards whom we feel a responsibility, who have been on our hearts during the last year, needing our love as Jesus needed that of his parents? We could thank God for the privilege of caring for them, and ask him to bless us in our dealings with them.

Lord, we thank you for your help throughout our lives.

WP

New Year's resolutions

I have come in order that you might have life—life in all its fullness.

Today is traditionally the time for making New Year's resolutions. I hate ones like 'I will eat less chocolate' or 'I will be on time'. They only make me miserable as I have as much chance of keeping them as a snowball has of surviving till July! I always blame myself for failing—as many women do?—and there are so many opportunities to fail these days! We set ourselves such high standards, and forget that God isn't bothered that we've made a less than perfect meal, or left dog hairs on the carpet which Great Aunt Flo is bound to notice. We get bogged down in details but God looks at the bigger picture, waiting to transform our lives into what they could be.

So how does this affect our New Year's resolutions? Well, whatever is worrying us most about the coming year is what we have to bring to God. I don't expect that it is really how much chocolate we eat! Family, relationships, money, job, moving, retiring, being over-busy, illness, ageing, becoming boring? The list of possible causes of anxiety can be very long, and I'm sure there are many more we could add. We need to invite God into these places, in our New Year's resolutions, claiming his vision of bringing us life in all its fullness.

So how about making the brave and risky resolution, 'I'll do my best to ask God into those areas in my life which are worrying me or that I know need changing'? Then leave it up to him. Maybe the answer will be a total surprise, like stopping trying to do so much, and starting to relax. Whatever it is, be on the lookout for God's peace and guidance.

Wherever we are, as midnight strikes tonight, could we silently pray for ourselves and for the world, asking God to bring life in all its fullness to us and to all people.

Lord, be at the centre of my 2001.

WP

DAY BY DAY WITH GOD

Magazine Section

Running on empty

Christine Leonard

It was an exhausting week. A kidney stone had become stuck in my husband's tubing (you don't want to know the details) and consequently my car became well acquainted with the route between our house and the hospital. Then, on the way to work one morning I found myself stuck in the worst traffic I'd seen for years. Pushed for time, this was all I needed. For some reason I glanced at the dashboard. My heart beat faster. The petrol gauge had swung so far into the red section that its needle leaned hard against the end stop. I thought I'd learnt my lesson in my first car when the engine spluttered to a halt in heavy rain and wouldn't do anything other than make a ticking noise. 'That's the petrol pump running on dry, you stupid woman!' my landlord had muttered as he'd rescued me. I'd never let the gauge sink below a quarter ever since… until now, with my mind on other things.

Panic and prayer

Adrenaline surges may assist flight or fight but they don't do too much for clear thinking. I broke into a sweat, picturing already-delayed motorists pushing my car out of the way. Where on earth was the nearest petrol station? The other side of the traffic jam. It took me a while to realize that I could turn round.

I prayed as I drove back home, then phoned work to say I'd be late and sat out the rush hour. What a symphony of delight when the expensive liquid finally splooshed into my tank!

I wish the solution to spiritual dryness were as simple. We can be so busy doing other things that it creeps in without our noticing. When we discover we're running on empty and our spiritual filling station—God—seems utterly inaccessible, how do we react? With panic, depression or anger? Do we feel a sense of failure, guilt or even indifference? In my current state of dryness I've felt all of these.

Church doesn't help much. Sermons often relate only marginally to real life. For example, we're coming to the stage where our ageing parents are going to need more and more help. One reason I started 'running on empty' was that two of ours had reached a crisis, but resisted any attempt to make their lives easier. So what do you do when you see someone clearly not coping? Do you respect their decisions or, feeling responsible, wrest control? With a two-year-old the answer's clear, but with elderly parents— what would Jesus do? I used up lots of mental energy trying to work it out—and upset everyone! Talking with friends, I realized that ours wasn't a unique dilemma but almost universal. So how come I have never, anywhere, heard good biblical teaching on the subject?

Parched

Then there's worship. I can make myself sing praise to God because deep down I know he never changes. He's always great and kingly and worthy of our praise. But, when dry, it seems hypocritical to participate in the kind of hymns or songs which go, 'God's good to me all the time and my faith in him increases day by day and whoopee, I feel so wonderful knowing him!' Looking around in church, I see a number of other non-singers, as well as many with rapt faces, lost in real worship. That, at least, is good. Psalm 73 talks about 'the circle of your children' and a church can and should act like a circle as each of us in turn helps to hold the others up. When I look at those who have been down but are now in a good place, I find at least some encouragement.

Realizing that almost everyone in our house group either felt low or was experiencing serious 'external' problems, I prepared a Bible study on dryness. I found all those verses about drinking the water Jesus gives and never thirsting again. They meant nothing at all. People who've known what it is to drink of Jesus clearly *do* thirst again! And then I found Psalm 143: 'My soul thirsts for you like a parched land.' Reading it together, our group decided that the psalmist was desperate, had been so for quite a while and that the cause was not primarily his sin. We asked why the Jews included such blistering honesty in their hymn book while the equivalent is missing in the worship repertoire of our churches? Why do most churches start their worship on a compulsory high note, rather than reaching our praise of and trust in God, as many of the psalmists do, from a low or difficult place?

When I asked the group what they found helpful in a time of dryness, the only reply forthcoming was, 'Reading Adrian Plass.' After a quick reading we did all feel miles better—because of our laughter but also because of Adrian's honesty. I wrote a new worship song—well, a metrical psalm-type thingy, to be precise. It begins, 'God, why is it so flippin' difficult being a Christian most of the time when my neighbours who don't tithe go on exotic holidays and their kids grow up really nice, unlike mine?' That helped too!

Psalmist's pain preserved

Positive effects of being dry have included a new respect for the Bible's honesty and relevance in passages like Psalms 42 and 73 and the book of Habakkuk. Psalm 88 remains in a gloomy place, ending with the words 'and darkness is my closest friend'. I'm not in *that* bad a state—but what a comfort to know that God chose to preserve the psalmist's pain in sacred scripture through the millennia!

My current dryness makes me appreciate the times when I have felt close to God. It has caused me to re-evaluate some of the things I'm doing and also to think hard about church—what is it for and what is my part there?

So, I expect you think I'm feeling better now, that my thirst's quenched and I'm all spiritual again! I should be. As I write, this is publication day for my ninth Christian book *and* a week when my notes for *Day by Day with God* are being read by the thousands of you who (unlike me) keep up to date. I've had a letter this morning from someone saying that a passing remark I'd made to her five months ago started something which has made a real difference to her life and work. But I still feel irritable, fed-up and demotivated—a real toe-rag, in fact. I found out what a toe-rag was the other day, while visiting London's rejuvenated Docklands. Loaders of grain used to wind rags around (you guessed it) their toes, to prevent the sharp chaff rubbing and cutting those appendages. That's me— prickly, hot and sweaty with effort and a none-too-fragrant aroma in the nostrils of the Almighty.

Preparing us for new things…

So, to conclude, the answer to spiritual dryness is… I don't know. I do know that I've been here before and emerged the other side to soak in God's love and grace. I do know that sometimes he creates this sense of dryness in order to sharpen our thirst for him and to prepare us for new things. I've experienced that before and I've a sneaky feeling it might be why so many at church are feeling dry right now. I do know that becoming all bitter and twisted or guilt-ridden, or giving up, won't help. I also know that, despite appearances sometimes, he holds me firmer than I hold him and that his grace is bigger than my weakness or desperation. And I'm 99 per cent certain that neither toe-rags, nor Christians running on empty, cause him too much of a problem.

God's touch

Beryl Adamsbaum

Have you ever risen early and gone out to watch the sun rise? Some years ago, during a mountain holiday in Switzerland, I did just that. I went out into a silent, grey world devoid of all colour... and watched one snowy peak after the other turn pink. I felt that the whole world was mine and that this magnificent spectacle was just for me. And yet, had I not been there, the sun would have risen just the same. It seemed to me that this glorious sight would have been wasted had there been no human eye to behold it. And yet God himself takes pleasure in the beauty of his creation. We sing, 'He has created all things and for his pleasure (probably more correctly *by* his pleasure—that is, according to his will—but the alternative translation is surely none the less true) they are created. Thou art worthy, oh Lord' (Revelation 4:11).

God's over-abundance

The glory of the sunrise, whether observed by human eye or not, spoke to me of God's over-abundance, of the lavishness of his giving. The Bible tells us that he gives not just life, but *abundant* life (John 10:10); he gives us all things *richly* to enjoy (1 Timothy 6:17); his love *surpasses* knowledge (Ephesians 3:19); the peace he gives *passes* all understanding (Philippians 4:7). And the psalmist exclaims, 'You have made known to me the path of life; you will fill me with joy in your presence, with eternal pleasures at your right hand' (Psalm 16:11).

It spoke to me, too, of another aspect of God's character. When I saw the peaks suffused in that rosy glow, I felt there should be some loud trumpet blast or some great acclamation to herald the new day. I couldn't believe that what was taking place before my eyes was happening so silently, so unobtrusively, in such peace and tranquillity. But isn't that just typical of the way God works? When he appeared to Elijah (1 Kings 19), we read that there was 'a great and powerful wind... but the Lord was not in the wind. After the wind there was an earthquake, but the Lord was not in the earthquake. After the earthquake came fire, but the Lord was not in the fire. And after the fire was a gentle whisper.' God revealed himself to Elijah in a 'gentle whisper' (NIV) or in a 'still, small voice' (RSV). And don't we still see God at work today in the same way, through his Holy Spirit in the life of a believer—quietly, discreetly? You might not even notice if you don't look in the right direction! Had I not actually been looking at the peaks in question, nothing would have told me about this glory that was unfolding in my very presence. Likewise, the results of the Holy Spirit's transforming work in the lives of God's children can be pretty spectacular as believers are changed into the likeness of Christ, or in terms of equipping and enabling for Christian service.

Transformed

Just as I stepped out into a grey world which was transformed by a touch of God's paintbrush, so our lives—which may be grey and drab—can be transformed into things of beauty by God's touch upon them.

More recently, I was in Australia, this time not alone, but in the company of a close and trusted friend with whom I have experienced times of precious fellowship and deep communion. Together, at the coast in New South Wales, we watched the sun rise over the horizon and shed a golden path of light across the ocean. The light and warmth of the sun's rays reminded us of God's holiness and love. 'In light inaccessible, hid from our eyes', this God, whose 'eyes are too pure to look on evil' (Habakkuk 1:13), has made himself accessible, by identifying with us sinners to the point of paying the penalty for our sin and dying in our place, because he loves us. As we contemplated the 'eternal light' as reflected in the rising sun, and remembered the offering and the sacrifice which opened up the way for us to enter God's presence, we marvelled anew that 'the sons of ignorance and night may dwell in the eternal light through the eternal love' (Thomas Binney).

Accepting the unacceptable

Sandra Wheatley

How many of us are where we would have imagined ourselves to be twenty years ago? How many goals have been met, how many hopes and dreams attained? If success is to be measured by such things, then I would be an abject failure.

A few years ago I thought I had it all—a successful job, involvement in a lively church, friends to enjoy life with and hopes still to marry, to have children, to settle down into blissful domesticity.

But one day all that changed—hopes became unhinged and life, no matter how much I tried, would never be the same again. I returned home from an emergency hospital visit with the words 'demyelination; multiple sclerosis' buzzing around in my head! It would have been far more acceptable if the consultant had said what I thought he should have said: all that was wrong was the result of overwork. I could have accepted that diagnosis and done something about it. But MS?

That night I wept and wept as I grieved for the loss of the life I had planned for myself—hopes and dreams all in tatters.

Lifestyle decisions

As the effects of the MS worsened, decisions had to be made regarding my lifestyle. Initially it meant practical things like moving house, changing my car—all 'coping' things, adjusting to the change imposed upon me. But all the while a battle raged within me, the battle to accept the unacceptable—to face up to the stark fact that it wasn't going to go away; the hospital hadn't made a dreadful mistake. Despite still having dreams in which I was able to walk and do all that I once did, I would wake up each day with something new to contend with—some other aspect of this disease that was affecting just about every system in my body. I had to move from 'coping' and 'adjusting' (badly) to finding acceptance.

I would spend hours poring over scriptures that spoke of Jesus healing the sick, and would talk with friends at church about healing. They would encourage me to continue to know 'that illness and disability are not God's will and that if you had more faith you would be healed'. Prayers would be prayed, and more and more I realized that I was becoming a disappointment to them as the illness got worse and my need to use a wheelchair increased. My involvement and inclusion lessened as long periods of bed-rest were needed.

It was during those times away from everyone, alone and isolated, that I began to see that I wasn't a disappointment to God. His promises to be with me in and through all that I faced were becoming more real as the days passed. The startling realization that nothing could separate me from him (Romans 8:38), including MS, were beacons of hope as my faith and my life were tossed about in a sea of uncertainty. I also heard the term 'harbour of acceptance' and struggled to find the reality. It wasn't easy. Acceptance was wrapped up in the notion of resignation and giving in to things. Friends at church questioned how I could accept and give in to this horrible disease. Others said that if I were to 'accept' it, wouldn't that mean that I was giving in to something that wasn't the Lord's will for me?

All the while, my awareness of God and the deep desire to know him meant that for me the most important thing was doing just that—knowing *him* was more important.

Challenge to trust God

I gradually moved closer towards the challenge to trust God when there was no outward sign or evidence that he was at work in my life. I realized that he loved me as I was—that his desire was to spend time with me and to let me know him. I gradually moved towards that 'harbour' and found that place of acceptance in him. Recently I read the story of the calming of the storm (Luke 8:22–25). Jesus begins with the statement, 'Let's go over to the other side of the lake.' With utter confidence the disciples jump into the boat and off they go. As I read it, I knew what would happen next. But then I began to wonder, would they have got into the boat if they had known what lay ahead—that a life-threatening storm would arise and that Jesus would sleep through it? I doubt that they would have set sail with him. Would I have got into the 'boat' with him and embarked on the journey I've had if I had known what would happen?

What of our lives? We aren't given a sneak preview, but we are given promises to uphold us and to encourage us to keep on going, even if it seems as if Jesus has gone to sleep! He has promised us a place of rest—a 'harbour of acceptance' where we see that it isn't about resignation and giving in, but about receiving and giving up—giving up to him all those things too difficult to contend with or to cope with. It is a place where our battered little boats can find calm waters, rest, refreshment and preparation for our next journey, our next voyage on to the sea of faith.

Acceptance of the MS has not been an overnight success story but with the acceptance of something seemingly unacceptable has come a peace that defies understanding—his peace and his presence that keeps me safe and holds me close.

Sandra Wheatley lives in County Durham, is a qualified nurse and was diagnosed with multiple sclerosis fourteen years ago.

Visit to a Second Favourite Planet

Hilary McDowell

Followers of Jesus are always 'just passing through', yet God wishes us to embrace the challenge of life on Earth to the full. Weaving together insights from Bible teaching with issues of daily concern, Hilary McDowell has written *Visit to a Second Favourite Planet* —a book peppered with a sense of humour and timeless insight. All those who have enjoyed *On the Way to Bethlehem*, BRF's 1998 Advent book, and Hilary's writing in *New Daylight* and *Day by Day with God*, will find fresh inspiration in her latest offering.

FROM THE QUARTERMASTER'S STORE

WELCOME BRIEFING

Welcome, Earthlings! So you are going to stay a while on the globe? There are a few things you need to know in order to enjoy and make the most of your time here.

First, congratulations. You have been allocated to one of the most beautiful planets created. The Maker took endless trouble over every small detail. The balance of life-sustaining elements, water, oxygen, atmosphere, even the precise angle of the tilt of the axis is positioned just 'so' in order to sustain life. He made a life support system second to none. Please try not to upset or destroy this finely balanced mechanism or the building blocks will collapse like a row of dominoes.

Your job will be a little more difficult because the Earth has already had some previous inhabitants who took all this for granted. It started with a couple called Adam and Eve. They disobeyed the Maker's instructions and bit into more than they could chew. My Boss, who is the Maker, gave them the choice, you see, because he hadn't created puppets. Unfortunately they made the wrong choice. It started a domino effect which exists even today. None of us can halt this momentum and it still continues, but we certainly can come 'on line' to the Maker's rescue plan to save Earth's inhabitants. Speaking of which, you are one, temporarily. The other aspects of his creation, the planets, stars, plant life, animals, sea and people, all come under the domino effect. In fact, just about everything you can imagine on the earth is slowly on a downward slide away from what it was originally intended to be.

Now this in itself doesn't sound irreversible. I mean, if the will is there, and with the right tools, it is possible to imagine folk saying, 'Maybe we could all pull together and…' But there is one small additional problem. Well actually, it is quite a considerable problem. Come to think of it, we are talking enormous obstacle—the Enemy. He's the one who originally tricked the first human couple into disobeying the Maker's instructions. Sorry to have to mention it, but he is still around, and he's mean, with a capital 'M'. The reason he is mean to Earthlings is that the Boss has no intention of letting him win the battle for Earth, but is only biding his time to let all new recruits to the planet choose whose side they want to be on before the axe falls. The Boss is fair that way.

I call the Enemy the 'Bad'Un'. Look out for him. He is not easy to spot because he does not want to be noticed. An undercover sabotage agent if ever there was one. It's better not to go searching for him. The Boss says there is no need to get jittery. But if you mean to stick around on the planet for a bit, you need to keep your eyes skinned.

Meanwhile, remember—the Boss intends you to have life here on the blue planet, real life, not just survival. So he is not about to abandon you. He will stick close, if you want him to. Adam and Eve weren't the only free people on the earth. It's your choice too!

EQUIPMENT CHECKLIST

Before advancing towards your assignment, please report to the supply store to check you are fully equipped for terrestrial habitation. You will require:

- One body in working order

- One brain in fully conscious mode

- One soul engaged in gear with the Maker

Please mark off each of these components with the official checklist and send me an order form if anything is missing. The sooner you discover a discrepancy, the better your chances for life and the quicker a deficiency can be rectified.

Body

Now, before I begin to receive a torrent of forms, I should just mention what is acceptable as regards the above three items issued. 'Working order' for a body entails that you must not be dead. It bears no relation at all to whether or not the body can fully see, hear, smell, touch, walk, jump, run or otherwise stagger around. The criterion of 'working order' owes nothing to the number of arms, legs, toes, hairs on the head or condition or prowess of the assembled parts. Please refrain from using any of the following methods to measure suitability:

- Standing in front of the mirror groaning

- Comparison of body parts with visual images on television, or in the written media, or with those of your peers who make fun of your 'bits', judging you inferior to their own condition

- Listening to the lie of the Bad 'Un who attempts to hoodwink you into believing that life and value are about perfection. He likes to taunt, often saying that you will never achieve such a state with your allotted body. He is right: you won't. No one has done. Value is not about perfection. Perfection this side of heaven is impossible. Life and value as a person are about knowing you are made in the Maker's image and he loves you.

Try pursuing that to its ultimate conclusion and you will not be requisitioning me for a new body.

Regarding the frustrations of wonky bits—everything from a big nose to a serious disability or illness—it might surprise you to know that the Boss says you are allowed to talk to him about such things. Complaints will be received graciously even though imperfections are not his fault. When logged into his two-way communication system, you will be amazed at his love and understanding. You may find yourself in receipt of a miracle, although this does not come on demand. Or he may surprise you with a novel way to cope. Or the item itself may turn out to be the kind of challenge which helps to revolutionize the world. Yes, yes, I do get a little melodramatic sometimes but that is because my own earth-type body issue was less than perfect. In fact it was quite seriously 'terrestrially challenged'. As a matter of fact there wouldn't have been a requisition form big enough!

I'd love to tell you what he did with it but I must not get distracted from the task in hand. It's sufficient to say that I believe that all things are possible in his strength. If he can work miracles in me, you have no problem. I would not be writing to you today as Quartermaster if he was not able to override the physical as much as any of the other imperfections of this globe.

Check your body: is it alive? Then it meets requirements for his powerful living.

Questions for group work or private meditation

What do you think of your body?

Who or what are you allowing to decide how you rate it?

Can you stand in front of your mirror and say, 'God doesn't make mistakes'?

If not, why not? Tell God what attitudes need changing.

Have you allowed God to begin working on your self-esteem?

Body-wise: List your strengths. List your imperfections. Which list is more difficult to write? Why?

Renewal

KEEP IN STEP WITH THE GOD WHO ACTS

Renewal is the leading Christian magazine with the charismatic edge. Terry Virgo says, '*If you want to stay informed, provoked and stimulated,* Renewal *is the magazine you cannot afford to ignore.*'

Each month *Renewal* offers:

- Swift, accurate news reports on worldwide revival and renewal
- Inspiring stories from the seemingly mundane but ultimately prophetic, through to the outright heroic
- Views: if our minds are being renewed—what are we thinking about comtemporary life?
- Resources: leadership guidelines; faith in the workplace; reviews; a shrewd Internet guide; musical instruments; Christian holidays
- Issues from your church: how can you win new converts? Would the cell church model suit your congregation? What's happening to your youth ministry? How can you empower the pews?
- Aspects of Christian faith and doctrine, emphasizing the work of the Holy Spirit

'*I thoroughly recommend* Renewal. *It is to the point, challenging and informative. Definitely worth reading*' - Maggie Ellis

Please see page 156 for subscription details

☩Wholeness

HEALTH FOR BODY, MIND AND SPIRIT

Wholeness is the only Christian magazine focused on the healing work of Jesus in its fullest sense, including emotional wholeness and spiritual growth.

If you are involved in any aspect of Christian ministry, particularly in counselling, pastoral care, healing, listening—or if you are seeking a fresh and nourishing spirituality—then this magazine is for you.

- Advice on all aspects of physical, mental and spiritual health
- Christian teaching on health and healing
- Hints on nutrition
- Focus on counselling
- Testimonies and interviews
- Prayers and meditations
- Details of retreats, courses and healing centres
- News of people, places and events
- Book reviews

'So many Christians struggle with physical or emotional problems and long to bring the love of God into the situation. Wholeness *will help you discover potentials you didn't know you had, and a God whose love is inexhaustible'* - Jennifer Rees Larcombe

Please see page 156 for subscription details

Renewal and *Wholeness* are published by Monarch Magazines a sister company to Christina Press

Other Bible Reading Fellowship titles

Advent Angels Sue Doggett
A host of stories, crafts, puzzles and things to do for the days of Advent
£3.99 in UK

George came through the front door of the school with his mum and his big sister, Stephanie. He didn't often use the main entrance and a tinge of excitement crept into his tummy as he entered the building. His nose was greeted with the smell of Christmas: pine-green needles and rich-fruited pies. His eyes widened at the sight of the tree with its shining baubles, coloured lights and nest of toys. His fingers traced the shape of the coins in his pocket.

The school fair marked the beginning of Christmas. George loved Christmas. And this year a very special surprise was waiting for him.

'It all started with just one angel and grew into a pocket full of angels,' said George.

Join in the fun with lots of stories, crafts, puzzles and games to enjoy throughout the days of Advent.

Visit to a Second Favourite Planet Hilary McDowell
…just passing through…
£5.99 in UK

'To be read by all prospective blue planet inhabitants on entering your new life as Earthlings. Please read your body instruction booklet, mind programming procedure and soul repair kit carefully, in conjunction with Maker's instructions. These are to be found in full in his book, which is a user-friendly manual designed to enable you to get the most from your time on the blue planet.'

Followers of Jesus are always 'just passing through', yet God wishes us to embrace the challenge of life on Earth to the full. Weaving together insights from the Bible with issues of daily concern, Hilary McDowell has written a book peppered with a sense of humour and timeless insight. It will refresh, instruct and inspire all who read it.

In the Beginning Stephen and Jacqui Hance
Bible readings for the first weeks of parenting
£6.99 in UK

The decision to have a baby is one of the most life-changing choices any of us will make. More demanding than getting married, more irrevocable than a career change, few of us quite appreciate what it will really be like until we have done it.

This book will enable people who have recently become parents to hear what the Bible has to say about raising children. It will help and encourage first-time parents and more experienced ones, biological and adoptive. It focuses on the joy and wonder of children, and the trials and challenges that they bring. It can be read by one parent alone or both together, in the first days of parenthood or later on.

'Very well arranged and full of practical advice. Parents—and babies in the long run—will benefit greatly.' *Sandy Millar*

'Mums and dads (especially new ones) need all the help they can get—and here is a book that sets them off on the right track.' *From the foreword by Ian and Ruth Coffey*

The Cost of Living Margaret Cundiff
A personal journey in John's Gospel
£5.99 in UK

The Cost of Living is a personal journey of discovery in the final chapters of John's Gospel, from the point when Jesus raises his friend Lazarus from the dead and then starts on the road to Calvary. In a series of accessible reflections, Margaret Cundiff delves into these chapters to help us discover what it means—and what it costs—when we choose to follow Jesus on this road.

The book of John is in many ways the most demanding, yet one of the best-loved, of the Gospels. Many Christians may be so familiar with the words that the great theological arguments behind them can be overlooked, while those reading for the first time may equally miss out on the deep truths. *The Cost of Living* provides an opportunity for both kinds of readers to encounter the Bible story afresh.

All the above titles are available from Christian bookshops everywhere, or in case of difficulty, direct from BRF using the order form on page 157.

Renewal  ✟ Wholeness

☐ Please send me a free
back issue of *Renewal*

☐ Please send me a free
back issue of *Wholeness*

SUBSCRIPTION FORM

When you subscribe to either *Renewal* or *Wholeness* for 12 issues
or more you will receive the following **FREE BOOK** (UK only)

Doughnuts and Temples by Erica White (worth £7.99)
- How to be nice to the body God gave you!

I wish to subscribe as indicated below (please tick):

Renewal (published monthly)   *Free books will be sent with these subscriptions

	United Kingdom	Europe	Rest of World
For 1 year	☐ £26.00*	☐ £32.00	☐ £34.00
For 2 years	☐ £46.80*	☐ £58.80	☐ £62.80
For 3 years	☐ £63.00*	☐ £81.00	☐ £87.00

Wholeness (published bi-monthly)

	United Kingdom	Europe	Rest of World
For 1 year	☐ £14.40	☐ £16.50	☐ £18.00
For 2 years	☐ £23.40*	☐ £27.50	☐ £30.50
For 3 years	☐ £33.15*	☐ £39.50	☐ £44.00

Name (Rev Dr Mr Mrs Miss Ms) _____

Address (BLOCK CAPITALS PLEASE) _____

_____ Post code _____

Telephone _____ Email_____

☐ I enclose a sterling cheque/PO payable to Monarch Magazines Ltd

☐ Please debit my Mastercard/Visa/Switch

☐☐☐☐ ☐☐☐☐ ☐☐☐☐ ☐☐☐☐ ☐☐☐

Expiry Date ☐☐ ☐☐   [If Switch Issue no _____   Start Date ☐☐ ☐☐

**Please return to: Monarch Magazines Ltd, Broadway House, The Broadway,
CROWBOROUGH, E Sussex TN6 1HQ or Telephone 01892 652364**

BRF Publications Order Form

All of these publications are available from Christian bookshops everywhere, or in case of difficulty direct from the publisher. Please make your selection below, complete the payment details and send your order with payment as appropriate to:

BRF, Peter's Way, Sandy Lane West, Oxford OX4 5HG

		Qty	Price	Total
016 2	On the Way to Bethlehem	____	£5.99	____
078 2	In the Beginning	____	£6.99	____
099 5	Advent Angels	____	£3.99	____
137 1	The Cost of Living	____	£5.99	____
144 4	Visit to a Second Favourite Planet	____	£5.99	____

POSTAGE AND PACKING CHARGES				
	UK	Europe	Surface	Air Mail
£7.00 & under	£1.25	£2.25	£2.25	£3.50
£7.10–£29.99	£2.25	£5.50	£7.50	£11.00
£30.00 & over	free	prices on request		

Total cost of books £ ____
Postage and Packing £ ____
TOTAL £ ____

All prices are correct at time of going to press, are subject to the prevailing rate of VAT and may be subject to change without prior warning.

Name _____

Address _____

_____

_____ Postcode _____

Total enclosed £ ____ (cheques should be made payable to 'BRF')

Payment by: cheque ❑ postal order ❑ Visa ❑ Mastercard ❑ Switch ❑

Card no. ❑❑❑❑ ❑❑❑❑ ❑❑❑❑ ❑❑❑❑

Card expiry date ❑❑❑❑   Issue number (Switch) ❑❑❑❑

Signature _____
(essential if paying by credit/Switch card)

❑ Please send me further information about BRF publications

Visit the BRF website at www.brf.org.uk

DBDWG0300   The Bible Reading Fellowship is a Registered Charity

Subscription information

Each issue of *Day by Day with God* is available from Christian bookshops everywhere. Copies may also be available through your church Book Agent or from the person who distributes Bible reading notes in your church.

Alternatively you may obtain *Day by Day with God* on subscription direct from the Publishers. There are two kinds of subscription:

Individual Subscriptions are for four copies or less, and include postage and packing. To order an annual Individual Subscription please complete the details on page 160 and send the coupon with payment to BRF in Oxford. You can also use the form to order a Gift Subscription for a friend.

Church Subscriptions are for five copies or more, sent to one address, and are supplied post free. Church Subscriptions run from 1 May to 30 April each year and are invoiced annually. To order a Church Subscription please complete the details opposite and send the coupon to BRF in Oxford. You will receive an invoice with the first issue of notes.

All subscription enquiries should be directed to:

BRF
Peter's Way
Sandy Lane West
Oxford
OX4 5HG

Tel: 01865 748227
Fax: 01865 773150
E-mail: subscriptions@brf.org.uk.

Church Subscriptions

The Church Subscription rate for Day by Day with God will be £9.75 per person until April 2001.

☐ I would like to take out a church subscription for _____ (Qty) copies.

☐ Please start my order with the January/May/September 2001* issue. I would like to pay annually/receive an invoice with each edition of the notes*. (*Please delete as appropriate)

Please do not send any money with your order. Send your order to BRF and we will send you an invoice. The Church Subscription year is from May to April. If you start subscribing in the middle of a subscription year we will invoice you for the remaining number of issues left in that year.

Name and address of the person organising the Church Subscription:

Name _____

Address_____

_____

_____

Postcode _____ Telephone _____

Church _____ Name of Minister _____

Name and address of the person paying the invoice if the invoice needs to be sent directly to them:

Name _____

Address_____

_____

_____

Postcode _____ Telephone _____

Please send your coupon to:

BRF
Peter's Way
Sandy Lane West
Oxford
OX4 5HG

DBDWG0300   The Bible Reading Fellowship is a Registered Charity

Individual Subscriptions

☐ I would like to give a gift subscription (please complete both name and address sections below)

☐ I would like to take out a subscription myself (complete name and address details only once)

The completed coupon should be sent with appropriate payment to BRF. Alternatively, please write to us quoting your name, address, the subscription you would like for either yourself or a friend (with their name and address), the start date and credit card number, expiry date and signature if paying by credit card.

Gift subscription name _____

Gift subscription address _____

_____ Postcode_____

Please send to the above for one year, beginning with the May 2001 issue:

	UK	Surface	Air Mail
Day by Day with God	☐ £11.25	☐ £12.30	☐ £15.00
2-year subscription	☐ £19.99	N/A	N/A

Please complete the payment details below and send your coupon, with appropriate payment, to **The Bible Reading Fellowship, Peter's Way, Sandy Lane West, Oxford OX4 5HG.**

Your name _____

Your address _____

_____ Postcode_____

Total enclosed £ _____ (cheques should be made payable to 'BRF')

Payment by: cheque ☐ postal order ☐ Visa ☐ Mastercard ☐ Switch ☐

Card no. ☐☐☐☐ ☐☐☐☐ ☐☐☐☐ ☐☐☐☐

Card expiry date ☐☐☐☐ Issue number (Switch) ☐☐☐

Signature _____
(essential if paying by credit/Switch card)

NB: These notes are also available from Christian bookshops everywhere.